**The Paris Codex:
Handbook for a Maya Priest**

THE PARIS CODEX

Handbook for a Maya Priest

BRUCE LOVE

with an introduction by George E. Stuart

AUSTIN

UNIVERSITY OF TEXAS PRESS

To Stephanie

and Matt and Jack,

and Eunice and Merton,

and Ed and Kale

Requests for permission to reproduce material from this work should be sent to Permissions, University of Texas Press, Box 7819, Austin, TX 78713-7819.

∞ The paper used in this publication meets the minimum requirements of American National Standard for Information Sciences—Permanence of Paper for Printed Library Materials, ANSI Z39.48-1984.

Library of Congress Cataloging-in-Publication Data

Love, Bruce, date
The Paris codex : handbook for a Maya priest / Bruce Love ; with an introduction by George E. Stuart. — 1st ed.
p.   cm.
Includes bibliographical references (p.   ) and index.
ISBN 0-292-74674-1 (alk. paper)
1. Codex Peresianus.   2. Mayas—Religion and mythology.
3. Mayas—Astronomy.   I. Title.
FI435.3.W75l68   1994
972.81′016—dc20   93-13028

Chapter openings: scribe carved in stone from Copan drawing by Barbara Fash.

Contents

CONTENTS

CONTENTS

Illustrations

Preface

This book began as a research project for a Junior Fellowship at Dumbarton Oaks Research Library in 1986. I had just finished my dissertation at UCLA under H. B. Nicholson, in which, among other things, I had tackled a glyph-by-glyph transliteration and decipherment of the texts in the Dresden Codex's New Year pages. I approached the Paris Codex in the same way, concentrating almost entirely on the glyphs, with little attention to the iconography or calendrics. Every glyph on every page was assigned its Zimmerman and Thompson catalogue numbers, and an attempt was made to assign phonetic or logographic values to every sign. This took the better part of five months. That, plus writing two articles for publication and attending numerous meetings, completed my stay at Dumbarton Oaks. I did not yet have anything close to a book.

That summer, with a grant-in-aid from the American Council of Learned Societies, I worked at George and Gene Stuart's house in Maryland, trying to flesh out chapters, but I found myself spending more time looking for a job than writing. As September 1987 arrived, I had no job and my wife and I decided to move back to California, where I again took up the honorable trade of framing houses. I then started my own contract archaeology business and slowly made the transition from pounding nails to writing cultural resource management reports for developers and engineers. By 1989, I had made enough money to take a summer off and return to my book. By a great turn of good fortune I was allowed, once again, to work at George and Gene Stuart's. There, surrounded by one of the best libraries in Maya studies anywhere, I wrote the present volume.

My focus had changed drastically, away from decipherment of hieroglyphs to a more (I hope) ethnographic approach to understanding how the codex was used by the Maya priest. To do this, I employed comparative materials from the Books of Chilam Balam and modern Maya ethnography, including my own fieldwork in various Mayan-speaking towns of Yucatán.

By early 1990, the book had been accepted for publication and the process of making revisions for the final draft began, a difficult process because in my work situation I was fairly isolated from the academic community of Mayanists. This situation happily changed when, in the fall of 1990, I received a position at the University of California at Riverside, where I divided my time between doing contract archaeology in Southern California and advancing my understanding of the Maya people of Yucatán, both past and present. In 1993, I left the university to establish a nonprofit research center, the Center for Indigenous Studies, where current work promotes Indian heritage projects in both southern California and Yucatán.

The only chapter to receive major revisions since the first draft is the chapter on the Maya constellations. This was totally rewritten in May 1992, based in part on the energetic and productive debates on Maya star lore presented the previous month at the Texas Maya Meetings in Austin. To those looking for a spate of new decipherments, this book will be a disappointment. But for those seeking an understanding of the integrative nature of Maya religion and the intricate interweaving of spirit forces as seen by the Maya priests, the book should be welcome. If it is received by students of the Maya as warmly as I have been received by those same people, the task of writing it will have been worthwhile.

Acknowledgments

It is humbling to realize how long is the list of people to whom I am indebted and without whom this book would be weaker by far. The list begins with Jim Fox and John Justeson, the only two "glyph people" on the West Coast in the early 1980s who understood what phoneticism is about. I was encouraged by Jim to present a paper at the AAA meetings in Chicago in 1984 in which I showed that the "nine Kan" offerings in the Madrid Codex were probably *bolon tas uah* "nine layered breads" based on modern agricultural ceremonies in Yucatán. That was my initiation into the exciting comaraderie of people dedicated to deciphering glyphs. I was warmly received by Linda Schele, David Stuart, David Friedel, David Kelley, Andy Hofling, and others who continue to share in the excitement to this day. To Linda and H. B. Nicholson I am indebted for their apparently strong letters of recommendation for the Dumbarton Oaks Junior Fellowship, where I was lucky enough to fall in with Karl Taube, Andrea Stone, and Flora Clancy. Karl, especially, shared his skills at iconographic interpretation, skills that are strengthened by his understanding of a broad range of Mesoamerican art, not just of the Maya. George Stuart allowed me to work on his Research Reports series where I spent many happy Saturdays. David Stuart, whom I got to know fairly well, amazed me, and continues to do so, with his absolute willingness to share his remarkable grasp on Maya writing. It was during this period that I got to know Floyd Lounsbury and Michael Coe, both of whom took time to talk to me and help me.

In the summer of 1989, when I was again writing at George and Gene's house, I was lucky enough to have John Carlson at hand to help me understand that elusive field known as archaeoastronomy. David Stuart again reappeared in my life just in time to let me bounce new ideas off him and, I hope, save me from some very embarrassing misreadings of glyphs. Gene, out of pure goodness, agreed to edit my first draft.

Back in California, Ed Krupp at the Griffith Observatory in Los Angeles gave me important insights on ancient astronomy that have led me to my most recent interpretation of the Paris Codex constellation pages, an interpretation that takes me away from the "zodiac" interpretation to the "signs of the night" interpretation generously given to me by Barbara Tedlock. Michael Closs and Victoria Bricker both have shown scholarly integrity and grace by sending me copies of published and unpublished materials even when I disagree with their findings. But probably more than anyone else I am most indebted to Karl Taube, who by luck or fate has been nearby when I needed to ask questions. He has so many times put me back on track when I was derailing. Dicken Everson, student of Archaeoastronomy, has helped educate me concerning planetary and stellar phenomena, and Amy Hoeptner has dedicated many hours to putting the illustrations together.

And then there are the Mayan-speaking people in the small towns of Yucatán where, through incredible openness and good will, I am allowed to sleep and eat and go to the milpa and play volleyball and record and photograph rites and ceremonies, all of which have colored my interpretation of the Paris Codex. The list goes on. To all the people at the Maya sessions at the AAA Meetings, the SAA Meetings, the Texas Meetings, the Philadelphia Maya Weekends, and the workshops—from the formal papers to the hubbub in the hallways and the dozens of restaurants—thank you all for letting me be a part.

Introduction
by George E. Stuart

The Paris Codex, or Codex Peresianus, has been perhaps the least appreciated and utilized of the four Maya hieroglyphic books now known to have survived the Spanish Conquest. The reasons for this are not difficult to understand.

First, the codex is short, the fragment of a longer original, and much of its content has been obliterated by time, particularly in the margin areas of the individual pages. Although the extant portion of the Grolier Codex, now in Mexico City, is even shorter than the Paris manuscript, the excellent preservation of the former makes it, by comparison, a veritable model of graphic clarity and completeness.

Second, it can be argued that the quality of draftsmanship in the Paris Codex falls far short of that which characterizes the Dresden manuscript, acknowledged for its beauty, clarity, and the intricacy of its content. This disparity is only exaggerated by the physical condition of the Paris pages. And while the Madrid manuscript may also be seen as the product of a mediocre draftsman, it at least possesses a certain raw vivacity and graphic impact which the Paris Codex lacks.

Third, the publication history of the Paris Codex has seen a succession of both primary and derivative reproductions and facsimiles of the manuscript that, on the whole, are not only quite varied in quality, but which are also rare and therefore difficult of access. Both factors have hindered all who have sought to investigate the codex in detail. As a result, there has been a relative lack of both specific decipherments and an interpretation of the Paris Codex as a coherent whole. The present study by Bruce Love does much to fill that gap. And since his treatment is fundamentally one of iconographic and epi-

graphic analysis, drawing appropriately on the efforts of past and present colleagues, I will confine the scope of the present introduction to simpler matters of the historical background and physical description of the document.

THE HISTORY OF THE CODEX

Of the origin of the Paris Codex we know nothing. It clearly originated in the Lowland Maya Area and, whatever the date of its actual painting, the manuscript as we know it was probably in use around the time of the Conquest.[1]

J. Eric S. Thompson (1972), Michael D. Coe (1989), and others have cited various early accounts mentioning Maya hieroglyphic books. Among these, Coe notes the narrative of Peter Martyr, who described the landing of Hernán Cortés on Cozumel Island: "Our people found themselves among unoccupied houses, and availed themselves of the food of the land, and found adornments of various colors in the houses, tapestries, clothing, coverlets of rustic cotton, that they call hamacas. They also have, O Holy Father, innumerable books" (Coe translation from Martyr [1944 : 325–326]).

Whether the Paris Codex was among these "innumerable books," some of which ended up as part of the "Royal Fifth" sent by Cortés to Emperor Charles V, we will probably never know. Whatever its provenience, the manuscript does not make its historical debut until 1832, when it was acquired by the Bibliothèque Imperiale in Paris. Günter Zimmermann, who has helped greatly in detailing the early history of the Paris Codex, speculates that it was among the Mexican manuscripts received by the library around this time from the collections of Baradere or Latour-Allard (Zimmermann 1954 : 62 n. 4).

In 1835 the artist Augustine Aglio drew the Paris Codex in the course of his ongoing commission—he had begun the task a decade earlier—to copy ancient Mexican manuscripts for Edward King, Viscount Kingsborough. The codex was to have appeared in the tenth volume of Kingsborough's *Antiquities of Mexico*—surely the most ambitious publishing venture in the history of Mesoamerican research. However, due to Kingsborough's death (in debtors' prison), that volume never reached print. Aglio's original rendering of the Paris Codex in its earliest knowable state is lost, but a first-generation version of it is preserved in a unique set of proof sheets on vellum, now in the famed Edward Ayer Collection at the Newberry Library in Chicago.

In 1849 the first known published reference to the Paris Codex appeared in a short descriptive text by Joseph M. A. Aubin (Anders 1968 : 9 n. 10; Glass 1975a : 179).

Late in 1855 Mexican scholar José F. Ramírez wrote a report on eleven codices in the Bibliothèque Imperiale. His description of the unprepossessing twenty-two-page Maya book (then Number 2 of the collection) noted its close resemblance to the Dresden Codex, which Ramírez had seen in the work of Kingsborough (1829–1848, vol. 3). The short commentary, relegated to the files of the library, did not appear in print for almost a century (Zimmermann 1954 : 63–64).

The efforts of both Aglio and Ramírez came to nothing in terms of publication, and notice of the existence of the Paris manuscript fared little better, although Aubin's (1849) mention of the codex was noted or quoted by Charles Etienne Brasseur de Bourbourg on two occasions (1852; 1857–1859, vol. 1). In 1859 José Pérez published two descriptions of the Paris Codex and illustrated one of them (Pérez 1859a) with a reproduction of a single page (Anders 1968 : 9 n. 10; Glass 1975a : 179; 1975b : 675). All in all, however, the first twenty-five years or so of the known existence of the Paris Codex constitute a kind of "lost generation," during which time the precious manuscript remained all but unknown to the world in general.

The codex was also apparently misplaced toward the end of that span. Late in 1859 the young Maya scholar Leon de Rosny found it in a basket among some old papers in a dingy and neglected chimney corner of the library. The codex was found wrapped in a now-lost paper bearing the word "Pérez"—perhaps a reference to José Pérez, who certainly must have handled the document shortly before.[2] Whatever the origin of the mysterious wrapper label, Rosny named the manuscript the "Codex Pérez" after it.[3] Despite the tardiness of his "discovery," the now-famous episode still pervades the historical literature as the marker of the beginning of the official history of the Paris Codex.

PUBLICATION HISTORY

The brief ephemeral publications of Aubin (1849) and Pérez (1859a; 1859b) on the Paris manuscript have been noted above. It is also appropriate to note the possibility mentioned by Glass (1975a : 179; 1975b : 690) that Rosny may have planned or actually produced a partial or whole publication of the manuscript as early as 1856, or *before* the date of his discovery (see Rosny 1856; 1860; 1864).

Whatever the resolution of the bibliographical tangle of the 1850s, the black and white photographic version of the complete Paris Codex published in 1864 by Minister S. E. M. Duruy and the Commission Scientifique du Mexique is generally recognized as the first edition (Glass 1975a : 179). Bibliographers disagree on how many of these were issued; estimates range from ten (Leclerq 1878) to fifty (Brasseur de Bourbourg 1871). Suffice it to say that the work, consisting of albumen prints pasted to paper sheets, is of superlative rarity. The quality and integrity of the 1864 images make them immensely useful to this day in visualizing the codex in its original historical state.

In 1887 and 1888, respectively, Rosny published color and black and white reproductions of the Paris Codex. Unfortunately, the color lithographic version was subject to some retouching, which damages its integrity. Ferdinand Anders (1968 : 21–22) notes the main differences between it and the 1864 photographs. Rosny's black and white edition of 1888 is excellent, and remains the best for details of the remnants of European script that appear on pages 9, 15, 16, and 19 of the original (see Appendix).

In his edition of the Paris Codex, William E. Gates (1909) transformed its pages into his characteristic format of redrawn conventionalized scenes with accompanying texts printed in the special Maya hieroglyphic font he developed. Gates included copies of the 1864 photographs with this edition.

Actual-size line drawings of each page of the codex, accompanied by matching explanatory layout diagrams, appeared in *Los Códices Mayas* by J. Antonio Villacorta and Carlos A. Villacorta (1930), the first combined edition of all the then-known Maya books. Although the work suffered from slight inaccuracies, it represents a truly awesome labor of draftsmanship (by Carlos Villacorta). Reprinted in 1976 and 1977, the work has proven to be the most durable and accessible working versions of the Maya codices ever done. The Villacorta version of the Paris Codex served as the basis for the manuscript as it appeared in the Russian compendium by Yuri V. Knorozov (1963).

Although the reproduction of the Paris Codex by Theodore A. Willard (1933) is based on photographs, the images were enhanced into starkly contrasting black and white line work, and the pages were printed on a screenfold that effectively replicates the form, if not the nuances and colors, of the original.

Since its publication in 1968, the facsimile of the Paris Codex done by the Akademische Druck- und Verlagsanstalt of Graz, Austria, has served as the standard. However, as Anders notes in the accompanying commentary, this facsimile is little more than a reprint of Rosny's 1887 color lithographic edition since it was not possible to make new photographs. For this reason, the Graz facsimile is accompanied by an excellent reprint of the 1864 photographs. This Graz color facsimile was copied directly for the 1985 printing of *Los Códices Mayas* by the Universidad Autónoma de Chiapas under the editorship of Thomas A. Lee.

The present edition of the Paris Codex utilizes the Ektachrome transparencies of the original manuscript in the files of the Bibliothèque Nacionale (formerly Imperiale) and were taken by the photographic staff of that institution.

DESCRIPTION AND PAGINATION

A complete description of the codex must at this writing be based upon the historical literature, for the manuscript itself is kept in a sealed container, inaccessible for first-hand examination.

The material of which the Paris Codex is composed was the subject of an investigation by Rudolph Schwede (1912), who based his conclusions on a close inspection of small fibers and fiber clusters taken from marginal areas of the original. Schwede's examination—the pertinent text of the rare work is reprinted by Anders (1968: 18–20)—determined that the base material of the manuscript was manufactured from the inner fibrous bark of the wild fig. The chalky material used for the sizing of this relatively coarse surface of yellowish-beige material eluded precise identification, but was thought not to be of mineral origin.

The draftsman of the Paris Codex employed some half a dozen colors in painting the manuscript. These include the basic black and red that dominate the palette, along with brown, pink, turquoise, and various blues. Some of the variation is doubtless due to the deterioration of aging. In its physical makeup the Paris Codex now consists of eleven vertical rectangular leaves forming twenty-two pages. These were originally joined together in screenfold, but the historical discrepancies in pagination (see below) suggest that some joined pages may have become detached—a problem difficult to resolve with certainty from the available page-by-page photographs. Both the obverse and reverse of the codex were painted. The average dimensions for each of the leaves are 12.5 cm. in width and 23.5 cm. in height. The calculated length of the unfolded whole is therefore around 1.40 m.

The pagination imposed upon the manuscript by various authorities has differed greatly since 1864, and a useful concordance of these diverse schemes has been compiled by Anders (1968: 41). The differences have come about because the content of the two "end" pages has been lost to almost total surface deterioration, confusing the issues of both subject matter and the number of leaves assumed to be missing.

The pagination employed in the present work matches that of the editions of Villacorta and Villacorta (1930; 1976; 1977), Anders (1968), and Lee (1985), which assigns the numbers 2 through 12 to the page sequence of one side of the codex, and the numbers 15 through 24, and then 1, to the other side. Pages 13 and 14 do not exist; their presence in the pagination scheme results from the general agreement that a now-missing twelfth leaf, which held these two pages back to back, once existed.

SUMMARY

The precious original of the Paris Codex remains where it came to light in the first place, in the Bibliothèque Nacionale in Paris, where it is catalogued in the *fonds mexicain,* Number 386 (formerly Number 2). The manuscript is sealed in a wooden case specially constructed so that two pages of it (20 and 23) are visible through a cover glass. We all owe a debt of gratitude to the venerable library for its custodianship of the Paris Codex.[4]

Given the great strides in the productive study of Maya and Mesoamerican iconography and epigraphy that have taken place in the past decade or so, the time is now ripe for a comprehensive study of the contents of the Paris Codex. That the moment has come is reflected in the recent appearances of interpretive works by Gregory Severin (1981), Hannelore Treiber (1987), and others on various aspects of the Paris manuscript. The present study by Bruce Love provides a much-needed comprehensive treatment that should serve as a baseline study for the foreseeable future. It should also do much in helping the Paris Codex at last take its rightful place among the great documents of ancient America.

Notes

1. Estimates of the age of the Paris Codex have ranged as far back as A.D. 1250, this based on stylistic resemblances to the Late Postclassic murals at Tulum and on the arrangements of the scenes on pages 2–11 to a stela at Mayapan (Thompson 1972:16).

2. Thomas A. Lee (1985:143) notes that additional words, in Tzeltal Maya, were also on the lost wrapper. This accounts for the use of "Tzeltal" or "Maya-Tzeltal" in the titles of some of the early commentaries on the Paris Codex (Gates 1909; 1910). Another result of this has been the attribution of the Paris Codex to the Tzeltal region of Chiapas (Villacorta and Villacorta 1930).

3. The name given the manuscript by Rosny has often led to an unfortunate confusion in the literature between the "Codex Pérez," meaning the hieroglyphic book in Paris, and the identical label applied to the miscellaneous collection of Colonial Period Yucatec documents and chronicles named for Juan Pio Pérez. The latter was first published by Solís Alcalá (1949).

4. The two visible pages of the Paris Codex formed part of the exhibition Aztlán, Terre des Aztéques: Images d'un Nouveau Monde, held in 1976 in Paris during the International Congress of Americanists' hundredth-anniversary meeting. A short description of the manuscript appears in the show's catalogue, edited by Le Rider (1976).

PART ONE

Background

1

Maya Books in Their Cultural Setting

The art of Maya writing probably developed in brush and paint before it was chiseled into stone. From ancient cultures throughout the world the shape and style of written characters reflect the materials used in their early development; those cut in stone or embossed in clay tend to be linear and geometric, those drawn with pen and brush are more looping and flowing (Anderson 1969: 11). The Maya script, preserved in stone from the first millenium of the Christian era, has the appearance of calligraphy, elegant and decorative, surely a style born of brush stroke rather than chisel. From the beginning of Maya writing, scribes probably composed texts on paper or skins in the form of folded manuscripts, the book form known today as the Maya codex.

The earliest testimony to the existence of Maya books comes from Maya art and archaeology of the Classic Period. (Maya civilization had its roots in advanced cultures that preceded it and that were outside the Maya area proper. Classic Maya civilization extended roughly from A.D. 250 to 900. The period between the end of the Classic Period to the arrival of the Spaniards in the early 1500s is known as the Postclassic. The sixteenth through the nineteenth centuries are roughly defined as the Colonial Period.) Several surviving Maya pottery vessels bear images of scribes with their codices (Coe 1977). In one scene (Fig. 1.1) a rabbit is portrayed painting in an open codex bound in jaguar skin in the palace of a Maya lord (Coe 1973: 90–93). In archaeological contexts, scribes loom large in the Copan monumental carvings (Fig. 1.2) at what is probably a regal scribe's residence (Fash 1989). Scientific excavations have revealed tantalizing remains of decomposed bits of painted stucco, perhaps the remains of books (Kidder 1937: 112), as in the spectacular 1989 discovery of a scribe's tomb at Copan (Fash 1991: 147–149).

The decipherment of artists' signatures and the glyphs for "write" and "carve," and indeed the title "scribe" (Stuart 1989), has reinforced the archaeological evidence for the preeminent status of Classic Period masters of calligraphy, but the social context in which books were used is still elusive. Scribes held an elevated position and their books were entombed in lavish crypts; yet beyond this, scant detail comes to the art historian or archaeologist about how the books were used. Fuller knowledge comes from ethnohistoric and ethnographic sources. (Ethnohistoric sources are documents produced by the Spaniards and other foreigners during the first centuries of occupation in the New World. The most complete record of sixteenth-century Maya culture in Yucatán comes from Bishop Diego de Landa. His *Relación de las cosas de Yucatán* is the quintessential sourcebook for students of the Maya. Ethnographic sources are modern eyewitness studies carried out by anthropologists and other field workers, like the classic work *Chan Kom: A Maya Village* by Robert Redfield and Alfonso Villa Rojas.)

In sixteenth-century Yucatán there was a clear distinction between the role of native political ruler (lord) and priest. In one part of the country, the high priest Ah Kin Mai was held in great respect by the lords, receiving gifts and offerings from them (Tozzer 1941: 27). While the lords were dedicated to economic and political affairs, the priests absorbed themselves with "sciences and ceremonies . . . as well as in writing books about them" (Tozzer 1941: 27). Clearly Maya sa-

Figure 1.1. Rabbit scribe writing in a codex bound in jaguar skin (Coe 1973:92). Courtesy of Michael Coe.

Figure 1.2. A scribe carved in stone from Copan, Honduras (Fash 1989:55; drawing by Barbara Fash). Courtesy of Dumbarton Oaks.

cred books belonged to the priestly class.

Maya priests throughout the provinces and towns of Yucatán maintained, manipulated, and directed the religious activities of the people. A far-reaching network of priestly knowledge was in place; books and the skills to use them emanated to the outlands from the great centers of learning.

In Mayapan, in the mid-fifteenth century, the high priests trained and taught students from surrounding towns: "[they] provided them with books, and sent them forth" (Tozzer 1941:27). From the white stone power centers to the forested farming hamlets, ritual and festival, music and dance, prayer and incantation surrounded and nurtured the people, unifying them, embracing them in a complex spiritual web of science and ceremony. Chief navigators through the crosscurrents of supernatural forces were the priests, guided by sacred books.

What were the sciences and ceremonies contained in these manuscripts? They were calendrical computations, divination and prophecy, prescriptions for rites and ceremonies, and history (Thompson 1972:5–12). How were they used? A rare eyewitness account from sixteenth-century Yucatán, recorded by Landa, provides the following detail.

During the month *Uo* the priests . . . began to prepare by fasts and other things for the celebration of another festival. . . . Having assembled, clothed in their ornaments, at the house of the lord, first they drove away the evil spirit as usual; then they took out their books and spread them out on the fresh boughs which they had for this purpose, and invoking with prayers and devotions an idol named Kinich Ahau Itzamna, who they say was the first priest, they offered him gifts and presents and burned before him their balls of incense with the new fire. Meanwhile they dissolved in a vessel a little of their verdigris with virgin water, which they said had been brought from the woods where a woman had never penetrated. With this they anointed the boards of their books so as to purify them. This having been done, the most learned of the priests opened a book and looked at the prognostics of that year, and he manifested them to those who were present. And he preached to them a little, recommending to them the remedies for their ills, and he assigned this festival for the following year to the priest or lord who was to celebrate it. . . . (Tozzer 1941:153–154)

As Landa described, a priest bore his holy book, bound in carved and decorated wooden slats, to the house of the principal lord where he staged a ceremonial reading of the inscriptions. An exorcism of malevolent spirits cleansed the air, leaving the sweet smoke of copal as ritual attendants prepared a leafy bed of moist green branches. He carefully laid his book on this freshly fixed matting and sprinkled it with hallowed droplets of virgin water. When all was ready he opened the book and pronounced the omens for the coming year.

Scenes like this were played out by the thousands through the lands of Yucatán in the centuries before the Spanish Conquest. But the cataclysmic onset of Spanish rule and the Franciscan zeal for religious conversion forced native religion underground. Possession and use of hieroglyphic books was punished by torture and death, and manuscripts were destroyed. Diego de Landa burned "a large number" around the year 1560 (Tozzer 1941:76–79). Landa's book burning and the ghastly inquisition trials held in the town of Mani in 1562 underscore the tenacity and persistence of native religious practice.

But Maya books and the practice of writing them survived in two forms. In their pre-Hispanic form—screenfold pages with glyphs and pictures—the books endured in the hands of Maya priests who refused to convert. Sometimes the priests clandestinely secluded the books within the very towns where Franciscans ruled, sometimes the books escaped with Maya people who fled to the hinterlands. The Itzá Maya of Tayasal, in modern Guatemala, maintained sacred books in their original format for a century and a half beyond the founding of Mérida, the modern capital of Yucatán. Perhaps that tradition ended at Tayasal, perhaps not, but today no evidence exists of any modern Maya retaining the skills of hieroglyphic writing.

Maya codices also survived by transforming. The Spanish hierarchy, eager to spread their religious teachings to the native population, instructed elite native converts in reading and writing not only Spanish but the Mayan language. Soon after the Conquest, Mayan-language vocabularies and grammars appeared; catechisms and religious doctrines were written in Mayan using the Spanish alphabet, adapted for the sounds and tones of Mayan speech. The same Maya intellectuals, Maya of noble descent who understood pre-Hispanic books, were the first to become literate in Spanish. They became official interpreters and schoolteachers—the new intelligentsia. Among them, however, were practicing subversives, believers in tradition who risked brutal retribution to pursue a form of cultural treason. They wrote—and therefore preserved forever—the "sciences and histories" from the ancient hieroglyphic books.

These books, written in the Mayan language using Spanish characters, are known today as the Books of Chilam Balam. Only a handful are known to have survived—perhaps a dozen. Examining these, scholars have shown without question that the books represent a continuation of pre-Columbian knowledge, an extension of native learning spanning centuries. Based on signatures, dates, and other internal evidence, the surviving Chilam Balam books were produced during a period spanning from 1544 to 1811 (Barrera Vásquez 1948:21). Although the various texts demonstrate ever-diminishing mastery of the ancient calendar and an increasing intermix with European ideas, it is significant that the scribal tradition itself persisted.

Given the millenium-long survival of scribal practice, is it so remarkable to find it functioning in the twentieth century? In the isolated forest hamlets of Quintana Roo in the 1930s an ethnographic study by Mexican anthropologist Alfonso Villa Rojas found such a tradition not only alive but absolutely vital to cultural solidarity:

> . . . Attended with a certain mystic prestige, are the secretaries or scribes. There are only two in the whole subtribe and as they are the only persons who know how to read and write Maya, their presence is essential whenever this special knowledge is required. In the meetings of the chiefs, for example, when some written message must be read or composed, the secretaries assume the principal role and their opinions are received with great respect. These men have in their keeping the correspondence of the group and those documents called Holy Books (*Santo Huun*), which consist of almanacs, printed booklets of Catholic doctrine and catechism, a copy of the Bible and some manuscript notebooks written in Maya. . . .
>
> Of these manuscripts the most important is a copy made in 1875 of an earlier document bearing the date 1628. The text of this document is almost identical with a section in The Book of Chilam Balam of Chumayel . . . entitled "The Interrogation of the Chiefs". . . .
>
> The secretaries keep all these books and papers well wrapped up in cloths and well put away in a safe place. . . .
>
> The secretaries enjoy a high social position. At the most important ceremonies and feasts they sit apart in a special place beside the principal chiefs. . . . (Villa Rojas 1945: 73–74; cf. Villa Rojas 1978:215–219)

In addition to participating in public ceremonies and feasts, the scribes of Quintana Roo were consulted in private. Individuals seeking weather forecasts, crop predictions, omens, and auguries sought the scribes' unique and esoteric skills. This type of personal consultation continues today.

In the 1980s, in eastern Yucatán, near Valladolid, three men arrived at the house of a village *hmen,* a ritual practitioner and modern native priest, seeking guidance about one of their wives, a very sick woman. The *hmen* brought out an old book, yellowed and brittle, and removed and unfolded a large sheet of numbers and signs. It was a divinatory manuscript published in Mexico City called *El libro de los destinos*. With this, he counseled the worried visitors (Love, unpublished field notes, 1983). Maya priests before Columbus probably received visitors in the same way, as councilors and men of knowledge.

SUMMARY

The Paris Codex was a sacred manual that conferred great status upon its owner. It empowered the Maya priest to see, as if through a crystal, the orderly workings of the universe. In the following chapters, an attempt is made to reconstruct a portion of that Maya world, to peer through the pages of the Paris Codex into the underlying belief system below. The codex itself is but a fragmentary relic, an artifact, but it helps us understand the cultural setting in which it was used. It reveals the ancient Maya spirit world, the priestly world of gods and other unseen forces—a world that could be understood and therefore controlled, or at least influenced, by those few practitioners skilled in the ritual arts.

2

Age and Provenience

Trying to determine the age and provenience of the Maya codices has intrigued scholars for most of this century. The approaches include examining internal evidence provided by the writing and any dates that may be present, matching astronomical events in the codices (such as eclipses) with real-world events, comparing art styles, and determining which Maya groups were most likely to have produced such books. One of the approaches not yet taken is a kind of common-sense consideration of the physical conditions under which the books were used, the setting in which Maya books were employed.

ETHNOGRAPHIC CONSIDERATIONS

While trying to discover the age of the Paris Codex, or any of the surviving codices, one must consider the cultural context in which it was used. These books were tools of the priesthood. They were consulted, perhaps daily, by the Maya ritual specialists for a myriad of purposes. In an eyewitness account from the early sixteenth century (see Chapter 1) a book was unfolded, laid on a bed of leaves, incensed, and sprinkled with sacred water in preparation for priestly consultation. Considering the constant handling, the continual opening and closing, and the transporting of books from the priest's quarters to the ceremonial temple, from the governor's palace to the outlying shrines, and even from town to town, one has to wonder how long a single book could survive. Coupling this wear and tear with the heat, humidity, torrential rains, and pervasive insect population of the Yucatán Peninsula, one gets a sense of the fragility of these manuscripts.

The books that were confiscated by the Spaniards and sent back to Spain were books that were currently in use in the sixteenth century. (The Grolier Codex is the exception; it was apparently found at an archaeological site by looters.) A collection of such books was found by Cortés and his party on Cozumel Island (Coe 1989) in a town that was inhabited by a native Maya population. The books burned by Landa and the testimony provided by numerous other early sources provide ample record to the great number of such books and their continued use even after initial Spanish occupation. Books could have been confiscated by soldiers or priests from almost anywhere in the peninsula throughout the sixteenth century and eventually sent back to Europe.

The question of dating the codices must take these points into account. They were in use at the time of Spanish contact and they were fairly fragile. This suggests that individual manuscripts could not have been in use for very long prior to their being confiscated. It is difficult to know how long a single book would normally last before wearing out, but one or two hundred years seems a generous estimate. Although texts and illustrations were copied and recopied for centuries, the individual books known today as the Paris, Madrid, and Dresden codices were probably produced within a generation or two prior to Spanish occupation.

ART TRADITION

One way to date the Paris Codex is to compare its art style with other art styles that have known dates. But the art tradition that produced the Paris Codex is not quite like any other. There are several complicating factors in trying to date the

Paris Codex based on art style. First of all, there are only three other Maya codices with which to compare it and they are all quite different in their art. A comparison of the Paris, Dresden, Madrid, and Grolier codices provides fascinating parallels in subject matter and format but produces little in the way of historical development of an art tradition.

There is a tradition of wall mural painting along the Caribbean coast of Yucatán for which many examples have been recorded and which can, to some degree, be dated. Arthur Miller (1982) has dated four phases of this tradition based on archaeological finds and changes in art style. The murals from Tancah Structure 44 show a drawing style most similar to the codices, in particular, the Madrid Codex (Fig. 2.1). The building has been dated by Miller to about A.D. 1350. But the Paris Codex style is really quite different. Among other things, the figures in the Paris Codex have distinctly long thin legs and broad midsections. Perhaps the most suggestive parallel comes from the Las Pinturas Group paintings at Coba, where a small fragment of a painted figure (Fig. 2.2) on Structure 2 reveals the lower legs and feet of a standing figure (Lombardo de Ruíz et al. 1987: Fig. 56; Taube 1989a: Fig. 5). Although the structure dates from the Late Classic Period, there are three layers of painting on it. The layer with the long straight legs is the most recent, but it is undated.

The Tancah-Tulum mural tradition was a regional tradition reflecting conventions followed within a limited area. Postclassic Yucatán was a mosaic of political and religious power centers. Even during the days when Mayapan extended a unifying effect on a large part of the peninsula, individual centers retained much of their autonomy and probably produced their own codices, even if only copies of existing books. Mayapan was certainly a major center of learning—priests were trained in the "sciences"—but sites like Izamal and Chichén Itzá were also centers of esoteric knowledge. Maní was another ceremonial center, in this case a pilgrimage center where Kukulcan was worshiped after the fall of Mayapan. In sum, the art style of the Paris Codex probably reflects a regional, limited tradition, a tradition that can be dated on archaeological

Figure 2.1. Figures from Tancah Structure 44 showing an art style similar to the Madrid Codex (Miller 1982: Plates 11–12). Courtesy of Dumbarton Oaks.

grounds only if examples are found in archaeological contexts that yield firm dates.

PROVENIENCE

There is some archaeological evidence that bears on the question of provenience and age of the Paris Codex. These are the stelae from Mayapan, the carved stones erected at that site during its period of power, A.D. 1200–1450. The stones were highly eroded and essentially illegible even in the sixteenth century. Landa gives the following report:

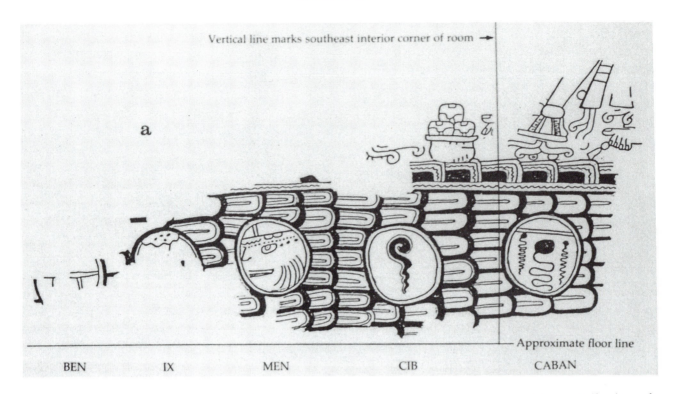

Figure 2.2. Drawing from Coba, Las Pinturas Group, Structure 2, showing feet and legs similar in style to the Paris Codex (Taube 1989a: Fig. 5). Drawing by George Stuart, a composite drawing based on Lombardo de Ruíz et al. (1987: Figs. 50–52) and unpublished 1:1 tracings of the murals made in 1975 by Gene S. Stuart. Courtesy of Center for Maya Research.

There are in the plaza of that city [Mayapan] seven or eight stones, each about ten feet long and rounded on one side, well worked and containing several lines of the characters which they use, and which cannot be read from their having been worn away by water, but it is thought that it is a memorial of the foundation and destruction of that city. . . . Natives, when asked about this, reply that they were accustomed to erect one of these stones every twenty years, which is the number which they used in counting their cycles. . . . (Tozzer 1941: 38–39)

In other words, the native population at Mayapan erected stones commemorating *katuns,* periods close to twenty years, and on these stones they wrote the history of that city.

By the time archaeologists reached Mayapan in the nineteenth and twentieth centuries, the stones that could not be read due to water ero-sion in Landa's time had deteriorated further. But one of the stelae was better preserved than the rest. Sylvanus Morley (1920:574–576), archaeologist for the Carnegie Institution of Washington, noticed some striking parallels between the Mayapan stela and scenes on the Paris Codex *katun* pages (Fig. 2.3). Proskouriakoff (1962: Fig. 12) later published a better drawing of it (Fig. 2.4). Morley calls it Stela 9; Proskouriakoff has it labeled Stela 1. Brasseur de Bourbourg (1867), the nineteenth-century French scholar, has also published a drawing of it (Fig. 2.5). Another stela from Mayapan, Proskouriakoff's Stela 9 (1962; Shook 1955: Fig. 4j), is a much more eroded, fragmentary stela, but it shows the same general composition and format as the better-preserved one.

Parallels to the Paris Codex are striking. There is a standing figure on the left with out-stretched arms and a seated figure on a raised platform. Between them is a 10 Ahau, a date des-

Figure 2.3. Morley's (1920:575) comparison of a Mayapan stela and a page from the Paris Codex. Morley labels it Stela 9.

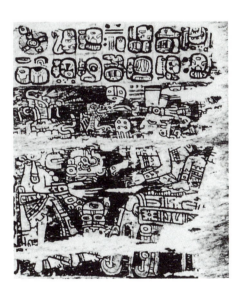

Figure 2.4. Comparison of a Mayapan stela and page 3 of the Paris Codex *katun* pages. The drawing of the Mayapan stela is from Proskouriakoff (1962: Fig. 12), where it is labeled Stela 1. Paris Codex courtesy of Phot. Bibl. Nat. Paris.

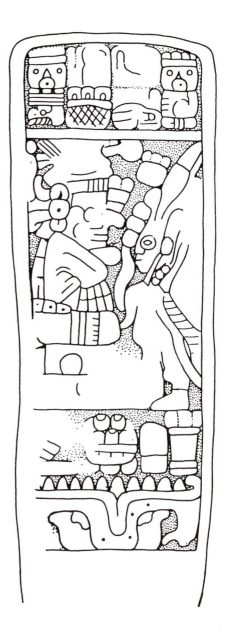

Figure 2.5. Brasseur de Bourbourg's (1867) drawing of the Mayapan stela.

Figure 2.6. A stela in the Campeche Museum that exhibits similarities in format and composition to the Mayapan stelae (unpublished drawing by Karl Taube after Mayer 1984 : Plate 62; 1989 : Plate 90). Courtesy of Karl Taube.

ignating a particular *katun*. A bird hovers above. The Paris *katun* pages, when compared with the Mayapan stelae, appear like a row of *katun* stones drawn on paper; or conversely, the Mayapan stelae seem to be pages from a codex transferred to stone. The similarity of the two is not proof that the Paris Codex came from Mayapan, but it is very suggestive. There is another stela (Fig. 2.6), in the Campeche Museum, that exhibits a somewhat comparable format and composition, but it is probably not from Mayapan (Mayer 1984: Plate 62; 1989: Plate 90). Perhaps it reflects the widespread influence of the Mayapan Confederacy in the Postclassic Period.

Mayapan was a center of codex production. Priests from outlying provinces came to Mayapan to be instructed in the "sciences" and were sent back to their towns with sacred books. At the fall of Mayapan, when the great center disintegrated, visiting nobles who had been residing there returned to their respective lands. Landa says their most prized possessions that they took with them as they abandoned the city were their books (Tozzer 1941:39). After the so-called Conquest, Spaniards were confiscating books throughout the Yucatán Peninsula. Any one of the confiscated books may have eventually made its way to Europe, but its point of origin may well have been Mayapan.

SUMMARY

At some point, the Paris Codex will be dated based on internal evidence. As shown in Chapter 3, there are historical events recorded on these pages by a series of numbered *tuns* (360-day years) falling within *katuns*. Presently, the precise reading of many of the glyphs is still uncertain, but as decipherment of the writing system proceeds, these passages will be read and understood. At that point, the age and provenience of the codex may become apparent based on the reading of the texts. Until that time, the best working hypothesis is that the Paris Codex was produced in Mayapan near the end of that city's existence as a power center, around A.D. 1450.

PART TWO

The Paris Codex

Pl. 4.

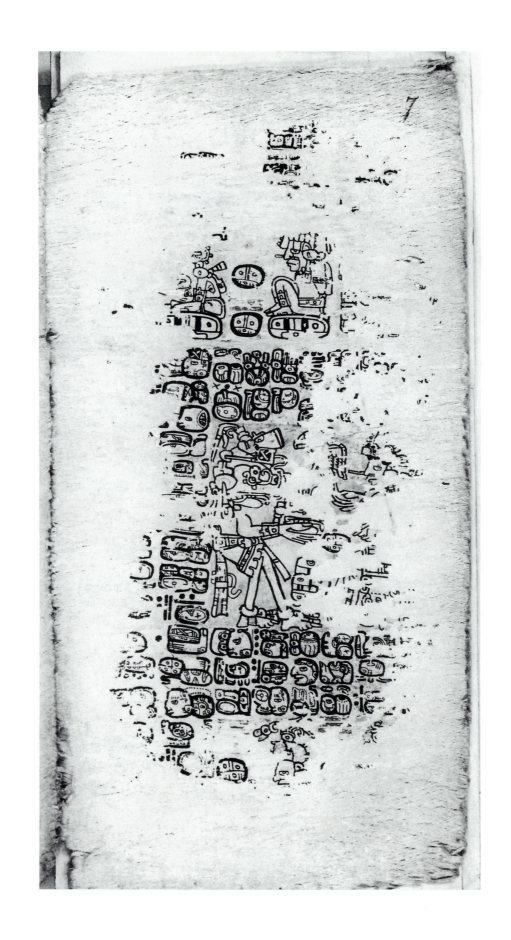

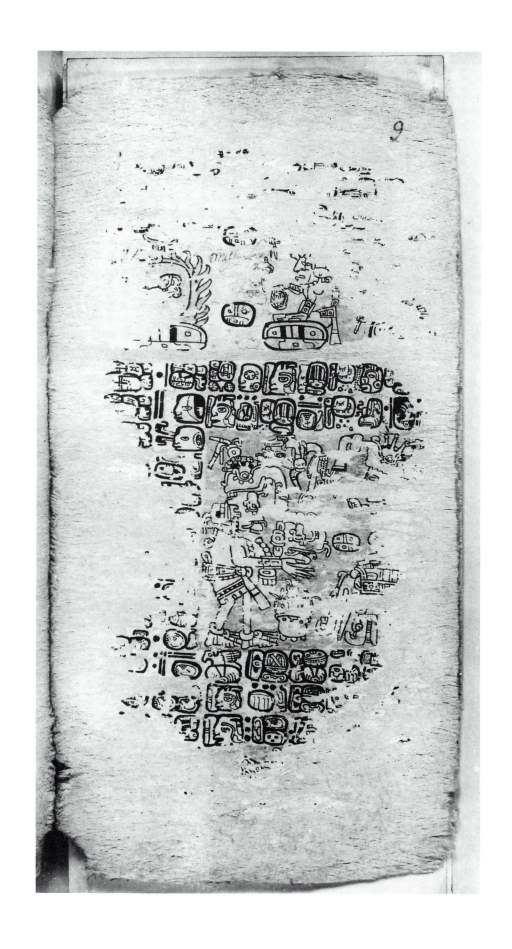

01

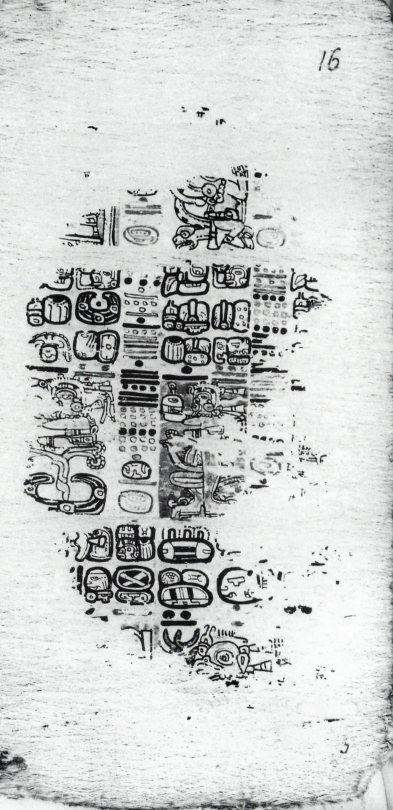

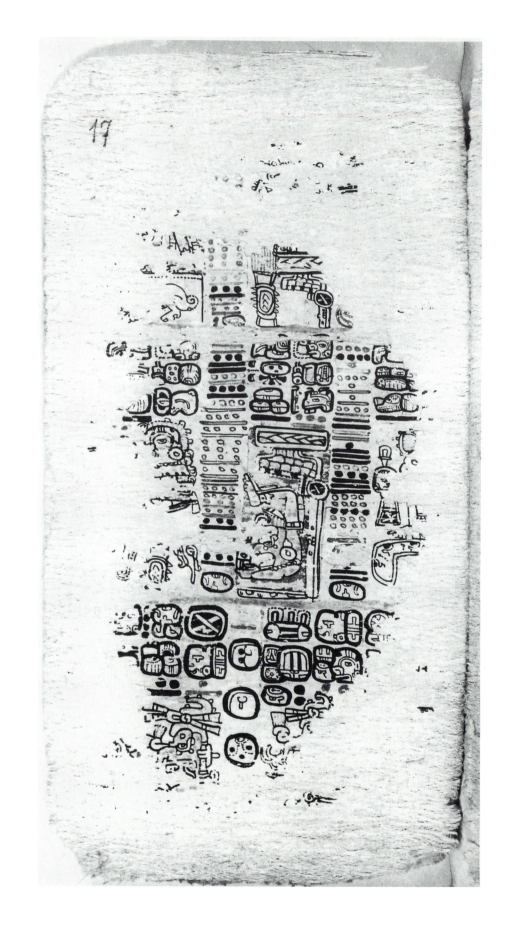

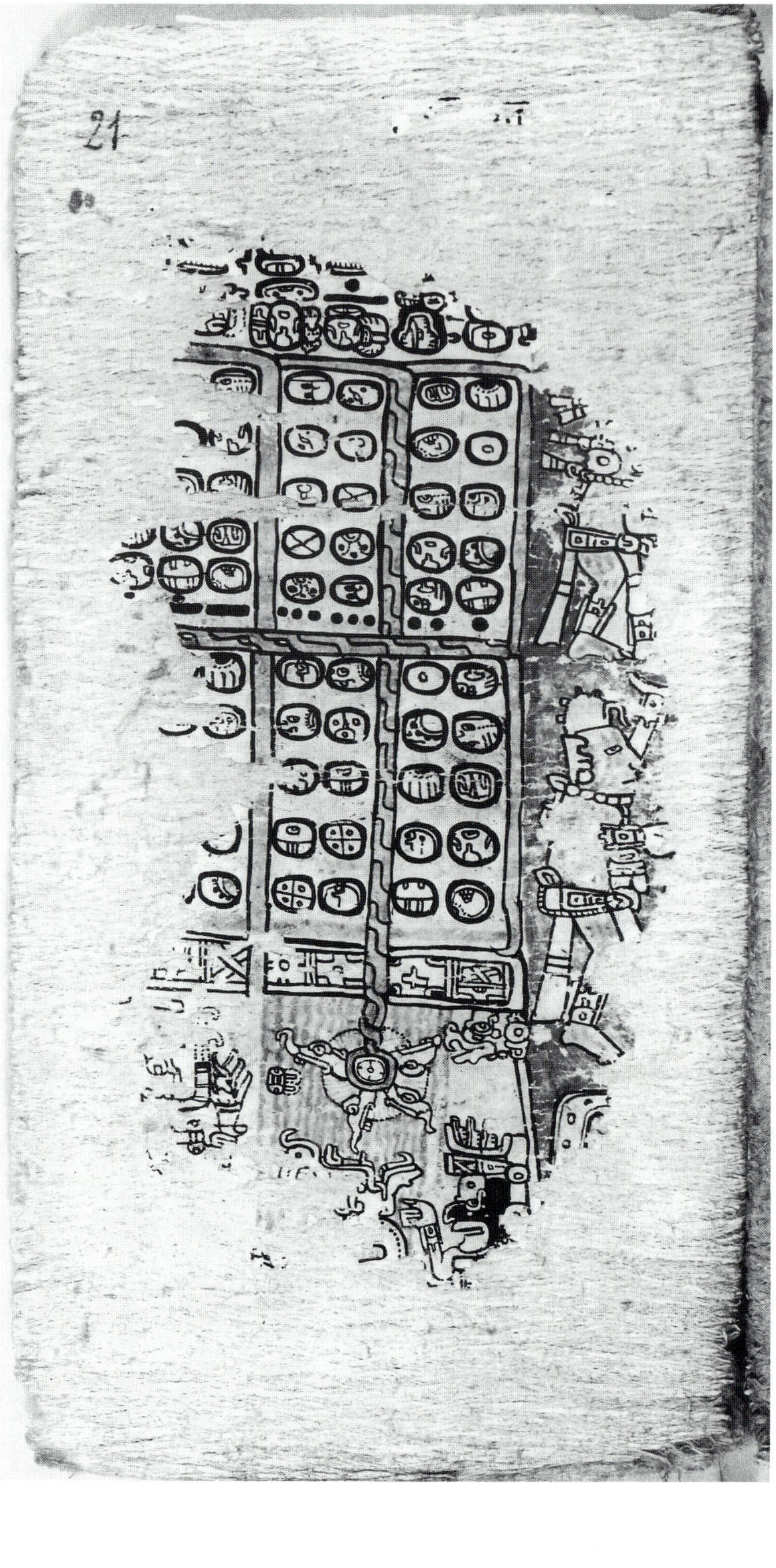
21

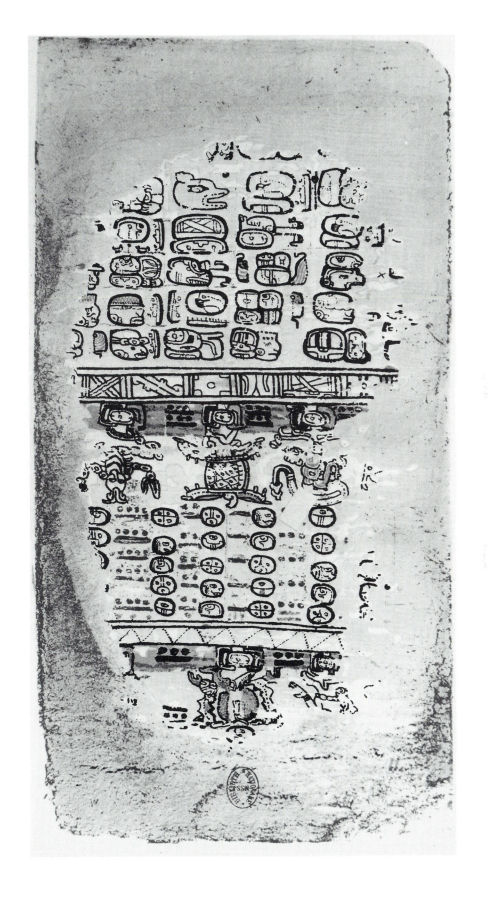

3

Katuns

Katuns are periods of time 7,200 days long; each *katun* is made of twenty *tuns,* which are periods of 360 days. In Late Classic and Postclassic Yucatán, *katuns* were the time periods essential and basic for recording history. The Long Count, the system of fixing dates which dominated the Classic hieroglyphic texts, was replaced by *katun* counts, a never-ending repeating cycle of thirteen *katuns*. Historical events were recorded by naming *katuns* and *tuns* within *katuns*. This practice continued up to and beyond the arrival of the Spaniards.

CONTENT

Katuns, like other Maya time periods, end on the day Ahau, one of the twenty Maya days. The *katuns* are named by the Ahau on which they end. The pages in the Paris Codex record a series of thirteen *katuns* beginning on page 2 with *katun* 2 Ahau (Fig. 3.1). Page 3 is named 13 Ahau, page 4 is 11 Ahau, and so on, following the standard numerical sequence for *katuns,* 2–13–11–9–7–5–3–1–12–10–8–6–4. Only the first ten pages of these are still visible, followed by the completely eroded page 12. There must have been at least two more pages in the original codex in order to complete the series. In European years, the period covered corresponds to A.D. 987–1244 or 1244–1500 (Barrera and Morley 1949 : Fig. 2).

The Paris *katun* pages are divided into upper, middle, and lower divisions with columns and rows of glyphs that span the middle and lower areas (Fig. 3.2). The upper division is the *tun-uinal* section, explained in the following chapter. The middle division is the *katun* section proper and is discussed in this chapter. The lower

division is extremely fragmentary and difficult to interpret.

The central element in the *katun* section is an illustration loaded with ritual information and ripe for interpretation by the initiated priest. The Lord of the Katun stands on the left holding his badge of office, the God K head. At his feet are the ritual offerings in a ceramic bowl. Above, the omen of the *katun* in the form of a bird hovers in space, while on the right, an elaborately costumed figure sits cross-legged on a bound caiman drooped over a high bench composed of a skyband with caiman heads for legs.

To the left of the picture are vertical columns of hieroglyphs running from top to bottom that declare the succession of the *katun* lords. On the far left is another column of glyphs, a single column apparently read independently. Only traces of glyphs in the far left column remain, but they appear to be not aligned with the visible double columns, indicating they were probably read separately.

Above the picture is a double row of glyphs eight glyph blocks wide that contain omens and auguries and *tun-uinal* dates.

Below the picture, beneath the feet of the *katun* lord and the caiman throne, are eighteen glyphs arranged six wide and three deep. These glyphs go with illustrations beneath them at the very bottom of each page. From the fragmentary remains it appears there are two figures with elaborate headdresses in each of these lower spaces (Fig. 3.3). Each figure is associated with a curious series of red bars, similar to Maya fives, but no dots are visible. Below the red bars are Ahaus, still visible on a few pages. There are also traces of a red oval shape (pages 4 and 5) of un-

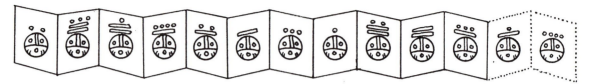

Figure 3.1. The thirteen *katuns* of the Paris Codex run from 2 Ahau to 4 Ahau. The bar-and-dot numbers are only visible on pages 3, 4, and 5; the other numbers, and the two missing pages at the end, are reconstructable.

known meaning that are also found in the *tun-uinal* Ahau columns (page 8) in the top register of these pages.

LORDS OF THE KATUN

In every scene there is a standing figure facing the center of the page and holding a God K head. The God K head serves as a symbol of authority, the Paris Codex counterpart to the Classic Maya "mannequin scepter." God K emerges from the ends of ceremonial bars in Classic Maya art (Fig. 3.4), which are clearly symbols of rulership (Spinden 1913:49–60; 1957). The ceremonial bar, or the God K effigy by itself, was passed from person to person as a power object bestowing the authority of kingship. Their interpretation as symbols of authority is widely accepted by students of the Maya (e.g., Robicsek 1978:59; Kelley 1976: Fig. 34).

At Palenque not only does God K mark rulership, it is directly associated with accession to office. On carved panels Lord Chan Bahlum, royal successor to the great Pacal, is shown holding the God K image (Fig. 3.5) and presenting it for public view in scenes of ritual and power (Schele 1976: Figs. 6, 10, 12). His accession date, 8 Oc 3 Kayab, is carved next to him, leaving little doubt that the scenes refer to his accession to office (Mathews and Schele 1974:66). This is important in understanding the Paris Codex. In the Palenque scenes, God K is not being passed, but is being displayed by Chan Bahlum as a mark of his authority within the context of his own rulership—his installation as lord. Following this model, the Paris figure can now be seen as also acceding to power; he is in fact the Lord of the Katun.

SUCCESSION TEXTS

As Lord of the Katun, the figure with the God K emblem is named at the head of a series of "lords" in the hieroglyphic texts to the left of the illustration. Seler may have been the first to see the rela-

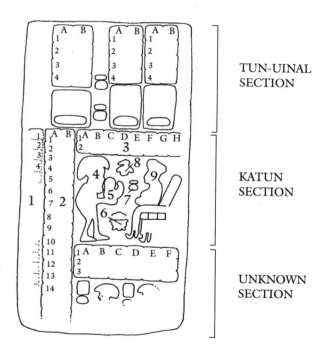

Figure 3.2. A typical *katun* page. At the top is a *tun-uinal* section. The bottom section, of unknown subject, has fragmentary figures and red bars and Ahau signs. *1,* single column of glyphs; *2,* double column of glyphs, succession and historical statements; *3,* glyphs of aspects and auguries with a numbered *tun* (and sometimes *uinal*); *4, katun* lord; *5,* God K symbol of authority; *6,* offerings; *7,* name of *katun*, a numbered Ahau; *8,* bird, omen; *9,* priest or chief.

RED
BARS →

↑
RED
OVAL
SHAPE   HEADDRESS   RED
↑   ↑   BARS
↑   HEADDRESS →

FRAGMENT OF
AHAU SIGN

Figure 3.3. Lower section of page 4. Courtesy of Phot. Bibl. Nat. Paris.

Figure 3.4. God K emerging from the mouth of a ceremonial serpent bar on Copan Stela N (Maudslay 1889–1902: Plate 82).

tionship of the illustrations and the glyphs (1902–1923:4:625–627, Eng. trans. 4:57). On several pages, the one-to-one relation is absolutely clear, as presented in Figure 3.6. As mentioned, the Lord of the Katun is only the first in a series of names, a series including either two, three, or four names followed by a smoking head with an infixed dotted Akbal sign. The smoking Akbal head always marks the end of the series.

Crucial to understanding the series is the "hel" glyph with the "swastika" that precedes each sign. Thompson (1950:160–162) first proposed the "hel" interpretation, a Maya word meaning "change" or "successor." He noted its use in the Paris Codex with the change of the *katuns*. Riese (1984) has thoroughly reviewed the glyph's usage in Classic and Postclassic texts, arriving at a general semantic interpretation of "change, termination, time." The Motul Dictionary meaning for *hel* is perfect for the Lords of the Katun series in the Paris. It reads, in part, "successor of whichever office or charge or that which succeeds or is put in place of that which is used up, removed, or missing" (Fig. 3.7). It can also be used as a verb meaning "to change" and thus takes a number of

affixes designating tense-aspect, number, person, and other linguistic variants. In the Dresden Codex New Year pages the *hel* glyph appears four times in the middle line of text dealing with the changing "gods" of the new year (Fig. 3.8). In all cases, it has the Ahau glyph over it, and twice it has the *ni* or *ne* suffix. The *ni/ne* suffix might well indicate it is to be read *helan* or *hela'an* "a thing changed or exchanged." (When the *wa* suffix is attached, as on page 26, the *wa* is a phonetic indicator for the Ahau glyph on top; when the *ni/ne* glyph is attached, the *ni/ne* is read with the *hel* glyph.) However, the *hel* translation can only be tentative for the codices because there are not enough substitution patterns with known phonetic glyphs to firmly secure the reading.

The text reads, "exchange rule 'Katun Lord,' exchange rule 'Katun Lord,'" etc. This reading fits well with an underlying concept described by Landa for the changing of the *katuns*. According to him, the Lords of the Katun were manifested in the material world as ritual idols that were incensed, worshiped, and then moved and replaced with the changing times. The exchange of *katun* idols, with a guest *katun* sitting in place next to

Figure 3.5. God K as a symbol of succession displayed by Chan Bahlum at Palenque on the Tablet of the Cross (Schele 1976: Fig. 6). Courtesy of Merle Greene Robertson.

the reigning idol, and the reigning idol only venerated during the first half of any *katun,* is a little unclear in Landa's description (Tozzer 1941:168–169), but the underlying principle of replacement and change is clearly reflected.

The final glyph in each of the succession phrases (Fig. 3.6) is a head with a dotted Akbal infix and smoke coming from its face. Taube has suggested (personal communication, 1991) that this glyph may be a form of God K, with an infixed mirror and smoke. If so, it is the glyph for

the God K head being held by the Lord of the Katun. The succession statement ends with "exchange rule 'God K.'"

FIGURES ON THE THRONE

Father Andrés de Avendaño y Loyola completed the final conversion of the Itzá Maya to Christianity in 1696 (Fig. 3.9). His observations from seventeenth-century Tayasal, in present-day Guatemala, add new dimensions to our understand-

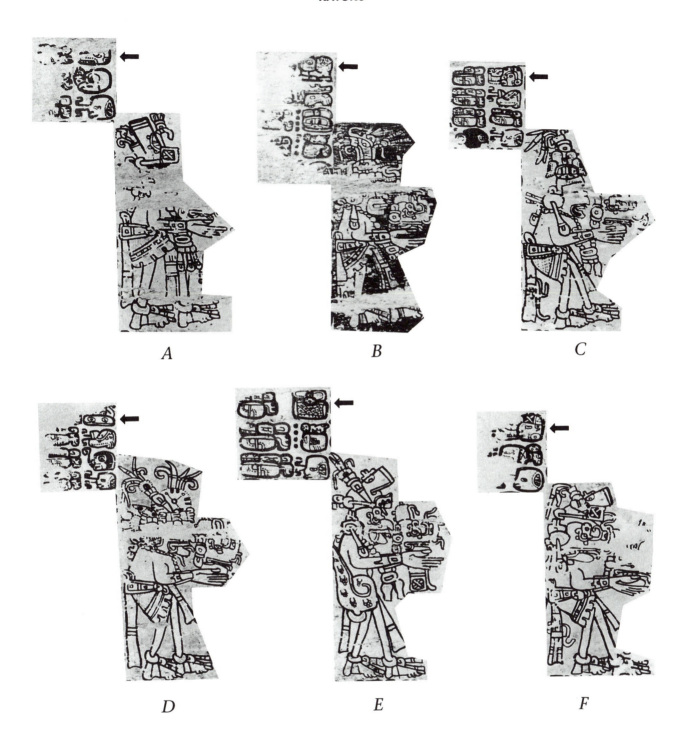

Figure 3.6. Katun lords. The name glyph of the standing figure is at the head of the succession list on the left. *A*, unidentified; *B*, unidentified; *C*, God C; *D*, unidentified; *E*, Pauahtun; *F*, unidentified; *G*, turkey; *H*, unidentified; *I, sip* "deer" (phonetic spelling *si-pi*); *J*, Itzamna. Courtesy of Phot. Bibl. Nat. Paris.

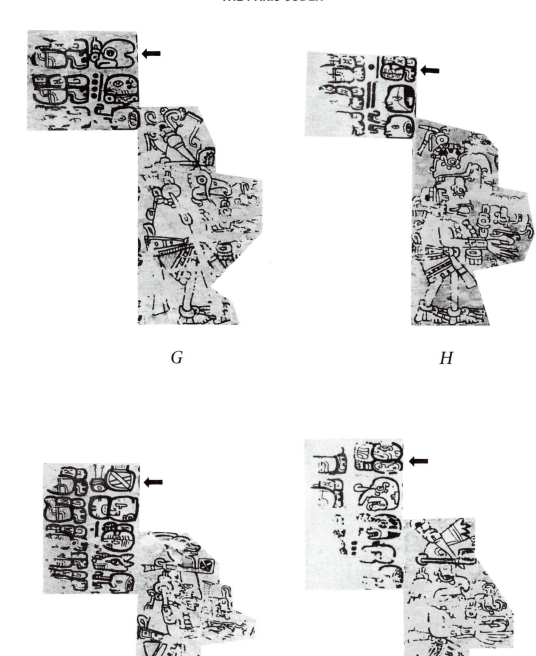

G

H

I

J

Figure 3.6. (continued).

Figure 3.7. Hel in the Motul Dictionary (Ciudad Real 1984:181v). Courtesy of the Coordinación de Humanidades, Universidad Nacional Autónoma de México.

Figure 3.8. Hel glyph in Dresden New Year ceremonies, pages 25–28. Courtesy of American Philosophical Society.

Figure 3.9. Map showing the Itzá territory around Lake Peten Itzá and the routes of various Spanish *entradas,* including Avendaño's of 1696 (Means 1917: Plate VI). Courtesy of Peabody Museum of Archaeology and Ethnology, Harvard University.

ing of *katun* rituals. Avendaño said that each *katun* had "its seperate idol and its priest, with a separate prophecy of its events" (Means 1917:141). In the Paris *katun* pages, if the standing figure is the Lord of the Katun, an idol of his image would be the *katun* idol referred to by both Landa and Avendaño. The hieroglyphic texts give the "prophecy of its events." Thus two of the three elements given by Avendaño are present, the idol and the prophecy. This suggests that the third element, the priest, may be the figure on the raised seat. If he is indeed the priest, then the illustration as a whole contains all the elements given by Avendaño: the idol, the prophecy, and the priest.

On four of the *katun* pages (pages 3, 6, 7, and 9) the faces of the figures on the thrones are wholly or partially visible, and in all cases they are those of humans, not gods. The throne itself has Classic Maya counterparts at Piedras Negras (Hellmuth 1987:298–299) and Naranjo, where people seated on thrones are real people—rulers of Classic Period sites or polities (Fig. 3.10). This suggests that the figures on the thrones in the Paris are real people, either priests or political rulers.

KATUNS AND POLITICAL GEOGRAPHY

The Maya, from their base at Tayasal, apparently controlled a considerable population. In Avendaño's report, the land of "Yucathan," the territory under Itzá rule, was divided into thirteen parts. *Katuns,* he said, ruled in succession in these thirteen subdivisions of the Tayasal polity: "Each age [*katun*], with its idol, priest and prophecy, rules in one of these thirteen parts of this land, according as they have divided it . . ." (Means 1917:141).

In northern Yucatán, just prior to the Spanish Conquest, the practice of moving the *katun* from town to town was a way of integrating Maya religion with political reality. A passage from the Book of Chilam Balam of Chumayel suggests that a *katun* stone, perhaps a stela or a carved altarlike stone, was set in place in different towns in successive *katuns*. A portion of the series reads:

Lahca ahau. te ch'abi. Otzmal utunile.
"Twelve Ahau there it was taken [to] Uxmal its stone."
Lahun ahau. te ch'abi. sisal utunile.
"Ten Ahau there it was taken [to] Sisal its stone."
Uaxac ahau. te ch'abi kan caba utunile.
"Eight Ahau there it was taken [to] Kancaba its stone."
Etc. (Gordon 1913:80)

This series runs through 11 Ahau, when the coming of the Spaniards was recorded in 1519. After that, the *katun* stone was no longer established.

Bolon ahau. mach'abi utunile lae.
"Nine Ahau not taken its stone there."
Uac [uuc] ahau. ma ch'abi u tunil lae.
"Six [seven] Ahau not taken its stone there."
Etc. (ibid.:80–81)

By the middle of the sixteenth century, centers of Spanish control were in place throughout the northern peninsula (Fig. 3.11), and public *katun* processions had ceased. But privately the records continued, recorded on paper by the Maya elite. The Book of Chilam Balam of Chumayel records a fifteenth- and sixteenth-century *katun* series showing that politics and geography were interwoven with *katun* commemorations; towns and polities received the sacred *katun* stone in succession, just as Avendaño would describe for the thirteen political divisions of Tayasal a century and a half later.

A *katun* wheel in the Chumayel document is a wonderfully graphic representation of time and space in Maya thought (Fig. 3.12; cf. Taube 1988a:198). As one follows the *katuns* around the wheel, one moves ahead in time while also passing through the directional coordinates: east, south, west, and north. At each station the *katun* is established, *u hets' katun,* at real towns or places—places such as *ich caan si hoo* "Mérida," *chi ch'een ytza* "Chichén Itzá," and *maya pan* "Mayapan." The figures seated on the thrones in the Paris *katun* pages, with their human faces, probably represent the priests or rulers of real geographical areas—the secular side of *katun* interpretations.

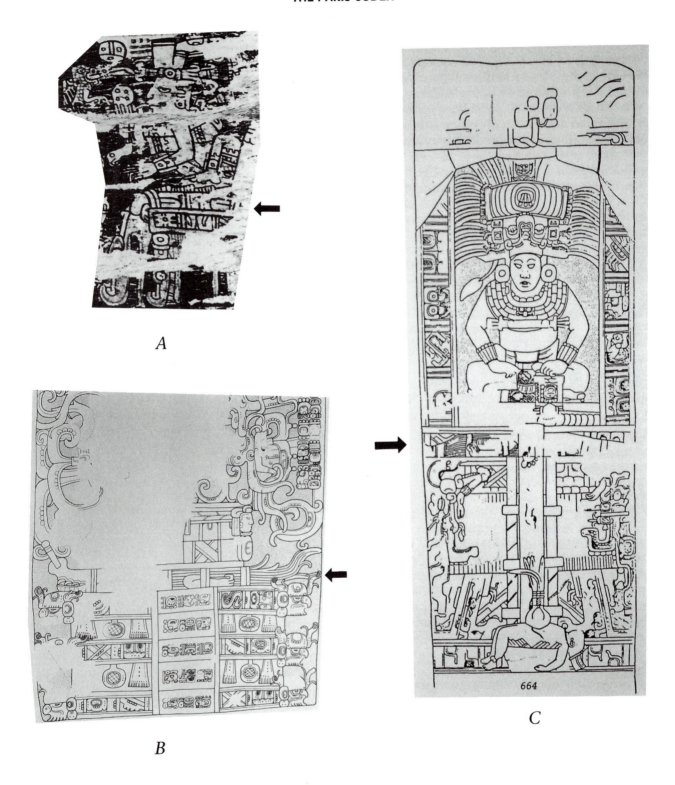

Figure 3.10. Caiman skyband thrones. *A*, Paris Codex, page 3; *B*, lower portion of Naranjo Stela 32 (Graham 1978:2:86); *C*, Piedras Negras Stela 11 (drawing by David Stuart, published in Hellmuth 1987:299). Paris Codex courtesy of Phot. Bibl. Nat. Paris; Naranjo Stela courtesy of Peabody Musuem of Archaeology and Ethnology, Harvard University; Piedras Negras Stela courtesy of David Stuart.

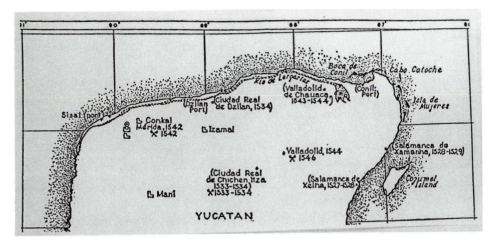

Figure 3.11. Spanish provinces and municipalities to 1550 (Chamberlain 1948: Map 2).

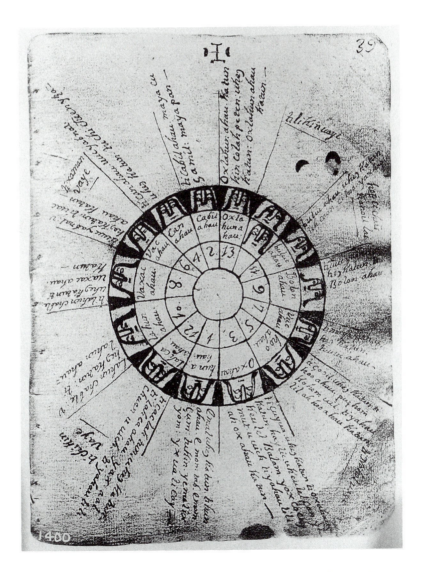

Figure 3.12. Katun wheel from the Book of Chilam Balam of Chumayel (Gordon 1913:72).

KATUNS AND HISTORY

Early Spanish writers were quite clear in stating that one of the principal functions of Maya books was to record history. Eric Thompson (1972:5–12) undertook a thorough review of the earliest Spanish sources and compiled an impressive list of rare, first-hand accounts of Maya books and writing. The Spaniards were repeatedly amazed and deeply impressed by the Maya ability to consult their histories of hundreds of years by means of strange signs in bark-paper books. As Avendaño wrote of the Itzá Maya at Tayasal near the end of the seventeenth century, their books ". . . show not only the count of the said days, months and years, but also the ages and prophecies which their idols and images announced to them . . ." (Means 1917:141). The "ages" were periods of twenty *tuns* known as *katuns,* as Landa explained from northern Yucatán in the sixteenth century: ". . . and by them they kept the account of their ages marvellously well. And thus it was easy for the old man of whom I have spoken in the first chapter, to remember (traditions) going back three hundred years" (Tozzer 1941:167).

HISTORICAL TEXTS

Even the earliest students of the Paris Codex recognized that the eleven visible pages on the front side of the codex represented a *katun* sequence (Rosny 1888:24–25). The Ahau numbers in the central illustrations on pages 3–5 form the sequence 13–11–9, the last days of three successive *katuns* (Fig. 3.1). The appearance of a *katun* sequence alone would indicate there is historical material involved, because *katuns* were the means by which the Postclassic Maya kept track of time and events. But several other clues within these pages also point to a historical interpretation.

There are *tun* signs with bar-and-dot numbers in the hieroglyphic texts above and to the side of the *katun* pictures. The logical interpretation is that these are *tuns* within the *katuns.* Several of these numbered *tuns* have a second set of bars and dots attached to them. Following the Classic Period model of suppressing glyphs for time periods, a numbered *tun* sign such as the one on page 6, with a three above and a twelve on the side, can be read as 3 *tuns,* 12 *uinals*

(Fig. 3.13B). During the Classic Period, in distance numbers, *uinals* and *kins* were often written in this way; the *uinal* glyph often has two numbers, above and on the side. One number was the number of *uinals* and the other number was the number of *kins.* The *kin* glyph was suppressed. In the Paris, the *tun* sign is shown and the *uinal* glyph is suppressed.

On every page except page 11 (where it has probably been erased), a numbered *tun* sign appears in the left-hand columns near the bottom of the text, sometimes with *uinal* coefficients, sometimes without. On five pages, the Ahau sign appears either one, two, or three glyph blocks later (Fig. 3.13). On the other pages, there are erased areas that may have had Ahau signs. On none of these Ahau signs can the number now be read with confidence, but they do have numbers—that much is clear. A numbered *tun* followed by a numbered Ahau is the clear Yucatecan method of recording dates—so many *tuns* within *katun* 3 Ahau, for instance (Thompson 1937; 1950: 197–203).

The consistency with which the numbered Ahaus follow the numbered *tuns* in the Paris pages in the left-side columns makes it almost certain that the texts deal with specific dates. If specific dates are marked within a hieroglyphic text, the reasonable interpretation is that they refer to historical events.

In the various Chilam Balam *katun* series, *tuns* are mentioned in the context of *katuns* when a certain important event occurs during a particular *katun,* as in the Chumayel series (Fig. 3.13D, E) referred to above. The Chumayel passage marks the abandonment of Chichén Itzá in the third *tun* of *katun* 1 Ahau: *tu yoxpis tun ychil hun ahau* "on the third *tun* within [*katun*] 1 Ahau" (Gordon 1913:79) and the arrival of the Spaniards in the seventh *tun* of *katun* 11 Ahau: *tu uuc pis tun buluc ahau u katunil* "on the seventh *tun,* 11 Ahau its *katun*" (ibid.:80). The "*tun*-Ahau" dates in the Paris, in the left-hand columns, probably record historical events.

KATUN PROPHECIES

In the Chumayel *katun* wheel discussed above (Fig. 3.12), as has been shown, several stations give the name of a town and a *katun* number, as

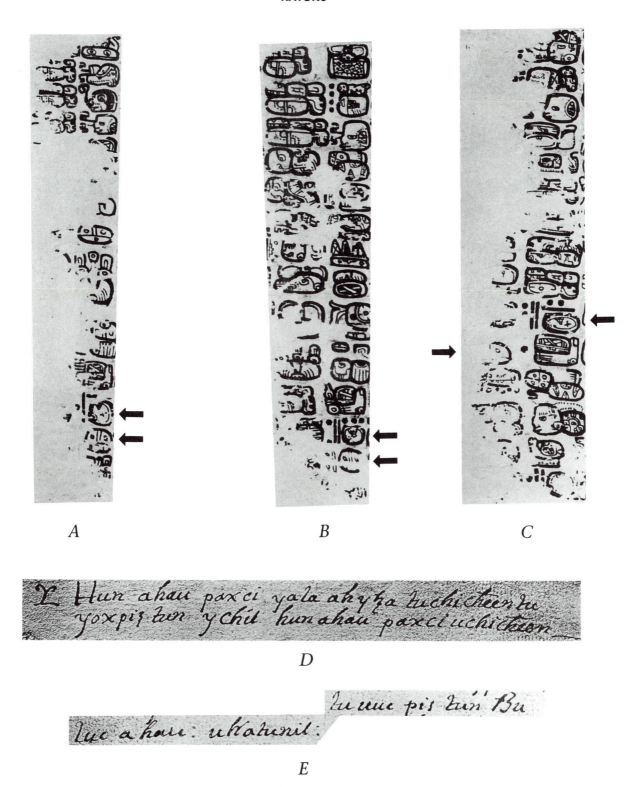

Figure 3.13. Tun-uinal-Ahau dates in the Paris *katun* pages and *tun*-Ahau dates in one of the Chumayel *katun* counts. *A*, Paris, page 5; *B*, Paris, page 6; *C*, Paris, page 7; *D*, Chumayel, page 79; *E*, Chumayel, page 80 (Gordon 1913). Paris Codex courtesy of Phot. Bibl. Natl. Paris.

in *Lahun Chable u hets' katun, ti lahun ahau,* "[at] Lahun Chable is established the *katun* at [*katun*] 10 Ahau"; but other *katuns* have additional information. For example, *Emal u hets' katun ti hun ahau* "[at] Emal is established the *katun* at [*katun*] 1 Ahau" is followed by *emom tab, emom sum, tu kin, yemal ix yom, yx ualicay* "descends the cord, descends the rope, on the day [sun?], descends the froth, 'ix ualicay [untranslated].'" It is lines like this that probably accompany the pictorial images on the Paris *katun* pages. The poetry, sound play, and metaphor of such passages has perplexed generations of researchers, producing a wide range of English and Spanish translations of the Chilam Balams. It is little wonder that the hieroglyphic texts of the Paris *katun* pages likewise resist decipherment.

On the page following the *katun* wheel in the Chumayel book there are four *katun* "prophecies" that read like condensed versions of more extensive texts found elsewhere. It is interesting to compare these with their longer counterparts in similar books. For *katun* 11 Ahau, for instance (Fig. 3.14), the Tizimin version contains everything included in the Chumayel but with many elaborations and additions. The Chumayel passage appears condensed to its crystalline core. Behind the carefully chosen couplets and poetic wordplay intertwined with calendrical and geographic details, one can sense the hieroglyphic writing from whence it came. It is lines like these that surely sprang from glyphic sources, sources like the Paris Codex.

On each of the Paris *katun* pages, the vertical columns of texts to the left of the picture begin with a succession statement, a series of *katun* lords. Near the end there is a historical statement—a *tun*-Ahau date. In between, in Maya sacred writing, lie the esoteric metaphors and ritual language forming the essence of Maya prophecy and divination. If modern students of the Chilam Balam books struggle with interpretation and differ widely in translation, it is no wonder the hieroglyphic passages defy translation.

PROPHECY TEXTS

The texts above the pictures are different from the texts on the side. Each has a numbered *tun* sign but, except for page 4 (discussed below), the *tun* sign is not followed by a numbered Ahau. The texts seem to deal with auguries and aspects, and in some cases follow a poetic coupletlike style of repeating phrases. Page 9 is a good example (Fig. 3.15). Very roughly paraphrased, it reads, "famine, —?—, Maize God; thrice-captured Maize God; death *tun*, death *tun*; twelve *tun*; death God C, death God K; —?—, —?—." This is not a historical narrative. The frequency of the *tun* signs, together with omens (in this case, bad ones), suggests that the texts deal with *tun* prophecies rather than *katun* histories. On page 6, a flint shield sign, the phonetic spelling of *ui'ih* "famine," and the *kin tun* signs "hot sun, drought" are remindful of the New Year prophecies from the Dresden Codex (page 26a) that give "flint blade year," "jaguar year," and "drought year" for the years beginning with the yearbearer Edznab (Fig. 3.15). These would be years filled with warfare, drought, and famine (Love 1991: 295–296), dire predictions indeed. While most of the texts in the Paris example are difficult to read phonetically, the gist of the interpretation is augural; they speak mostly of bad times.

The numbered *tuns* in the upper texts are problematical. They are different from the ones in the left-hand column of glyphs. They appear in the middle of the texts rather than at the end, and they are not followed by numbered Ahaus; they are not part of *tun*-Ahau dates. On several pages, the *tun* signs have two attached bar-and-dot numbers, above and on the side. These may be interpreted in the same way as the *tun* signs in the left column, as *tuns* and *uinals* (see above).

Page 4 is a special case. The numbered *tun* has a *sac* sign prefix and appears to be the month sign Zac. This is followed by a sign Akbal with a five or six attached. In turn, this is followed by a 10 or 11 Ahau. This phrase, "month sign, day sign, numbered Ahau," has been interpreted by Hannelore Treiber (1987) and others as a calendar round date, specifically 5 Akbal 16 Zac in *katun* 11 Ahau. If Treiber's interpretation is correct, the implications are very significant because the only occurrences of 5 Akbal 16 Zac in a *katun* 11 Ahau are during Classic Period times, 9.4.13.4.3 and 9.17.16.15.3 (Treiber 1987: 65). This would mean either that the text was referring to something

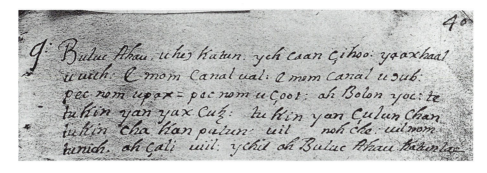

Figure 3.14. Two versions of a *katun* prophecy for *katun* 11 (*buluc*) Ahau. *Top,* Chumayel (Gordon 1913:73); *bottom,* Tizimin (Mayer 1980:21r). Tizimin courtesy of Akademische Druck- u. Verlagsanstalt.

which happened during Classic times or that the original version of this text was written during Classic times and copied into the current codex.

There are some minor problems with the calendar-round interpretation. First, the calendar round is written in reverse order. Normally the numbered day sign comes first, followed by the numbered month sign. It should read 5 Akbal 16 Zac instead of the other way around. Second, the number on the Akbal sign is attached to the wrong side of the sign; it should be on the front side instead of the back. Third, it is not clear what the coefficients are on the Akbal and the following Ahau sign. They could be 5 Akbal 11 Ahau or 6 Akbal 10 Ahau. These arguments are not completely damning to the calendar-round interpretation presented by Treiber, but they do give reasons for caution against uncritical acceptance of such a reading.

The hieroglyphic texts at the bottom of each page do not exhibit familiar patterns of grammar or syntax. They are sprinkled with deity names, verbs, and augury glyphs, but little more can be said about them at this time. They do not contain numbered *tun* signs.

SUMMARY

In sum, the glyphs of the *katun* pages are difficult to understand in detail, but certain general observations are valid. The left-hand columns begin with successions of *katun* lords and make historical statements using *tun*-Ahau dates near the end. The glyphs above the pictures have numbered *tuns* but not Ahaus (except on page 4). They are predominantly augural and have a coupletlike syntax. They appear to be prophecies for *tuns,* not *katuns.* The glyphs at the bottom do not have numbered *tuns.* No syntactic patterns

Famine,—?—, Maize God; thrice–captured Maize God; death year, death year; twelve *Tun*; Death God C, Death God K; —?—, —?—.

A

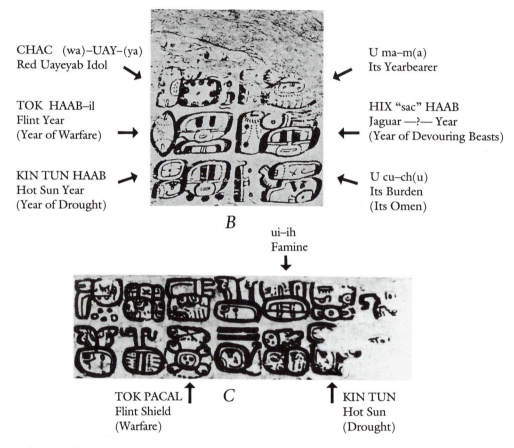

CHAC (wa)–UAY–(ya)
Red Uayeyab Idol

TOK HAAB–il
Flint Year
(Year of Warfare)

KIN TUN HAAB
Hot Sun Year
(Year of Drought)

U ma–m(a)
Its Yearbearer

HIX "sac" HAAB
Jaguar —?— Year
(Year of Devouring Beasts)

U cu–ch(u)
Its Burden
(Its Omen)

B

ui–ih
Famine

TOK PACAL
Flint Shield
(Warfare)

C

KIN TUN
Hot Sun
(Drought)

Figure 3.15. Augural texts from the Paris and Dresden codices, read in double columns, left to right. *A*, Paris, page 9; *B*, Dresden, page 26; *C*, Paris, page 6. Paris Codex courtesy of Phot. Bibl. Nat. Paris; Dresden Codex courtesy of American Philosophical Society.

are clear. They no doubt go with the pictures below them, which are almost totally gone. One very productive approach to deciphering the *katun* pages would be more intensive work with certain *katun* passages from the Books of Chilam Balam. They are arcane and difficult to translate, and they certainly will provide clues to the codex glyphs.

The Paris *katun* pages are extremely rich and full of meaning. They combine gods, humans, history, prophecy, and probably political geography. They contain the longest narratives of any surviving Maya codex but resist a clear reading by the modern student. In pre-Hispanic Yucatán, the never-ending series of *katuns* was the grand framework within which Maya life proceeded. The priest consulting these pages held in his hands the sacred guidebook giving him power to consult the past and predict the future, and make ultimate sense of life itself.

4

Tuns and *Uinals*

Tuns are periods of time consisting of 360 days. *Uinals* are 20 days long. *Tuns* and *uinals,* like the *katuns,* end on the day Ahau and are identified by the Ahau date; for example, a *tun* designated as 6 Ahau refers to the 360-day period leading up to and ending on the day 6 Ahau. Of course, these time periods were much more than ways of keeping track of dates. Each day and each period was loaded with supernatural significance; reading the calendar meant reading divine forces.

CONTENTS

Across the tops of the *katun* pages are figures seated on *tun* signs with two Ahau dates in the spaces between. On each page there are three visible figures on *tun* signs, and on all pages there is space on the left side where the painting has been lost. In many cases, there is room enough for another complete *tun* figure (pages 6 and 7, for instance), but elsewhere there are not enough spaces on the left side for more figures, and in those cases the leftmost *tun* has been widened as if to fill the area (pages 8 and 9, for example). There is a possibility that a missing column of glyphs could lie on the left side, but there is no evidence to suggest this. Thus, the unavoidable conclusion must be that the total count of *tun* figures and their complete original layout is unknown.

Above each figure lie the remains of a double column of glyphs which, upon close inspection, show evidence of having been four glyph blocks high, making eight glyph blocks over each picture. Many of the glyphs are reconstructable even where only tiny fragments remain because they are common signs found elsewhere in Maya manuscripts.

In the spaces between the *tun* figures are two Ahau signs, one atop the other, with bar-and-dot numbers. A close inspection of the spaces above them shows traces of drawings that were not Ahaus or bars and dots, as on page 5, above the 10 Ahau, where there is a trace of a football-shaped outline that at first glance appears to be the bottom part of an Ahau glyph. Measurements taken from one side to the other show that the sign is much wider than any other Ahau glyph in the whole *tun* section; and it is red when, if it were an Ahau, it should be black. On page 8, in the same place, another red sign appears, unidentified, but clearly not an Ahau or bars and dots. Above it is a black line, likewise not an Ahau. On page 9 some flecks of original paint near the top, in the Ahau column, are once again not the right shape or position to reconstruct an Ahau sign. The analysis of this section must therefore proceed on these findings: there are two Ahau dates, probably no more, in each column between the *tun* signs.

TUN SEQUENCE

The bars and dots on the lower Ahau signs can be read clearly on pages 3–8; but those on the upper sign can only be read on pages 5 and 8. Yet from these, the entire set can be reconstructed (Fig. 4.1). Beginning on page 2, the sequence, reading only the bottom Ahau signs, reads 3, 12, 8, 4, 13, 9, 5, 1, 10, 6, 2. The same sequence works for the top signs if one starts with 9 on page 2 and counts across the pages, using only the top signs, 9, 5, 1, 10, 6, 2, 11, 7, 3, 12, 8. The 10 and the 11 are the visible numbers on the upper signs on pages 5 and 8.

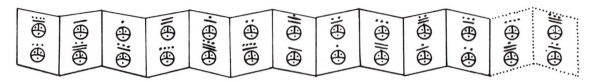

Figure 4.1. Reconstructed Ahau numbers for the Paris *tun-uinal* section, the upper division of the *katun* pages.

The number series, running horizontally from one page to the next, forms a typical *tun* sequence. Because of the mathematics of numbers 1 through 13 cycling with twenty day names, a *tun* ending on day 12 Ahau will be followed, 360 days later, by a *tun* ending on 8 Ahau, which in turn will be followed by a *tun* ending on 4 Ahau, and so forth. This sequence, coupled with figures of gods and animals seated on *tun* signs, leaves little doubt that this section of the codex is dealing with a *tun* series.

MAYA USES OF *TUN* SERIES

In searching to understand how the Maya may have used a series of *tuns* in a sacred book, one must turn to the Books of Chilam Balam for comparative material; to the ethnohistorical sources for eye-witness accounts; to archaeological sites for material data; and, in one case, to the Mexican codices. There are no comparable 360-day counts in the other pre-Columbian Maya books, but there is one in Codex Laud from Mexico (Fig. 4.2), which has been interpreted by Burland (1947; Martínez Marín 1961:18–19). There, on pages 39–46, a count of forty-five days is divided into eight stations various distances apart. Each station has a picture of a priest or god impersonator performing a ritual act. The series of forty-five days is counted eight times, bringing one back to the beginning of the table in a never-ending ritual count of periods of 360 days—in other words, *tuns*. The illustrations apparently indicate prescribed rituals performed in these periods.

In the Chilam Balam books, *tun* series seem to have received little attention compared with the years of 365 days. Calendar wheels and auguries of the yearbearers (explained in Chapter 7) pervade the Chilam Balams, but these fall within the context of the 365-day year, not *tuns*. *Katun* counts, both divinatory and historical, are widely known, and each *katun*, of course, consists of twenty *tuns*; but only occasionally are the *tuns* themselves recorded or their meanings elaborated.

Two such *tun* counts with accompanying texts are found in the Chilam Balams of Tizimin and Maní, but they are so alike that they undoubtedly derive from a common ancestor (Roys 1949a, 1949b). They record a series of *tuns* within a *katun* 5 Ahau, and there is an extensive, complex, and poetic treatise accompanying each *tun*. Roys (1949b:159) states, "Across these pages flits a shadowy procession of gods and monsters." Translations of these works, due to the esoteric language, are extremely difficult and far from secure, as can be seen by comparing the three extant translations (Barrera 1948:167–188; Roys 1949b; Edmonson 1982:69–112). There is a mix of divination—filled with evil times, hunger, and drought—and apparent real history including occupations of cities, warfare, and abandonments of places.

Within the Chronicle of Oxkutzcab, there is a short historical narrative covering the period 1534–1545, which includes the founding of Mérida (Morley 1920:471, 507; Thompson 1927:5–7). A typical entry gives the European year first, followed by a yearbearer date, the *tun* ending falling within that year, the *uinal* position of the *tun* ending, and some historical event or events. For example:

1538 anos bolo[n] kan ahcuch-hau tu hunte pop uchci chac-ykal u . . . hintah cimil lae uaxac ahau he tun tu uaclahun xul-e.

1538 years, 9 Kan the yearbearer on 1st of Pop, there was a great wind (hurricane) [causing?] death. There 8 Ahau the *tun* on 16 Xul.

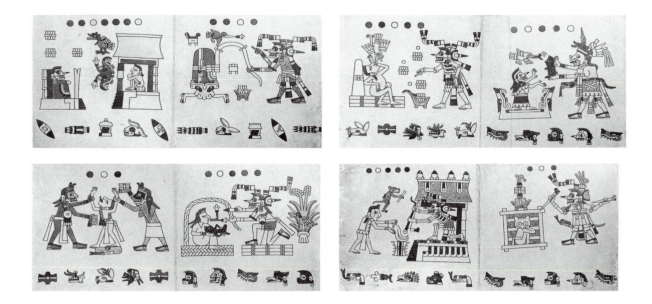

Figure 4.2. A *tun* count from Codex Laud, read from bottom right to top left (Burland 1966). Courtesy of Akademische Druck- u. Verlagsanstalt.

Note the *tun* ending 8 Ahau, followed by its month position 16 Xul. This brief chronicle meshes three Maya calendrical sequences—yearbearers, *tuns,* and *uinals*—with European years to provide a framework within which historical events could be told.

Tatiana Proskouriakoff (1952) discovered another *tun* count in the Códice Pérez (which has been miscopied by Solís Alcalá [1949 : 246], followed by Craine and Reindorp [1979]). It covers the years 1758 to 1774 (Fig. 4.3). It has a similar format to the Oxkutzcab count given above, but without historical events, and it includes some additional data. It begins with the European year, followed by the yearbearer and 1 Pop, and ends with the "month" date for the *tun* which falls in that year. In between lies a column of *uinal* numbers, a column of Ahau signs without numbers, and a running set of day signs from 9 Ix to 2 Ben. The *uinal* numbers are discussed below. Proskouriakoff points out still another *tun* count, though terribly jumbled, in the Chilam Balam of Kaua for the years 1797–1824. The point that Proskouriakoff emphasizes is that the count of the *tuns,* marked by the "month" dates at the end of each entry, had survived, remarkably into the nineteenth century.

To summarize, two *tun* counts, in the Tizimin and Maní, deal with omens and auguries meshed with history, while two other *tun* counts, in Oxkutzcab and Kaua, lie within brief historical counts of European years.

If *tun* prophecies were important to the pre-Hispanic Maya, there is surprisingly little evidence for it in the Spanish historical documentation. One ceremony described by Landa, however, may have been just such an event; performed during the month Uo, a priest with his hieroglyphic codex interpreted the signs and gave a "sermon" on the prognostics for the current or coming year (Tozzer 1941 : 153–154). Thompson (Roys 1949b : 159) has pointed out that in 1553, perhaps the year of the ceremonies described by Landa, a new *tun* would have started in the month Uo, so the "year" for which the priest was giving a reading was really a *tun.* Other than this less than explicit data, Maya *tun* prophecies are absent from Spanish accounts.

Archaeologically, the Santa Rita murals from the east coast of the Yucatán Peninsula have some intriguing parallels to the Paris *tun* series (Fig. 4.4). This unusual example of late Postclassic art portrays some twenty-three human or godlike figures in various postures and costumes, many

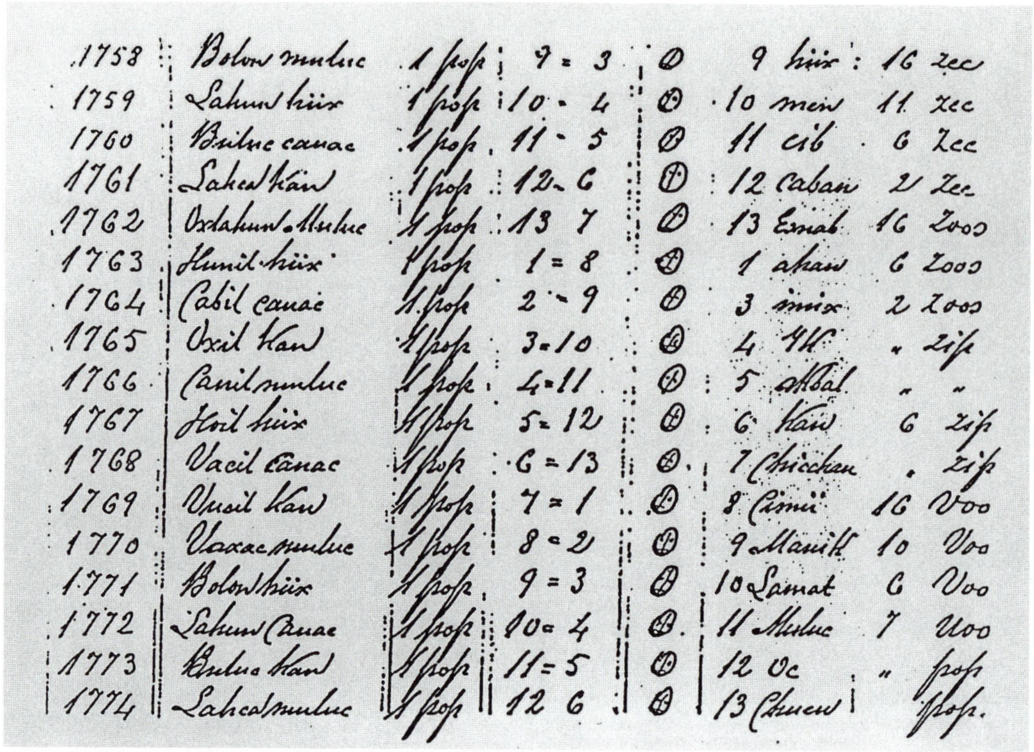

1758	Bolon muluc	1 pop	9 = 3	⊕	9 hiix	16 zec
1759	Lahun hiix	1 pop	10 - 4	⊕	10 men	11 zec
1760	Buluc canac	1 pop	11 - 5	⊕	11 cib	6 zec
1761	Lahcal kan	1 pop	12 - 6	⊕	12 caban	2 zec
1762	Oxlahun muluc	1 pop	13 7	⊕	13 Eznab	16 zoo
1763	Hunil hiix	1 pop	1 = 8	⊕	1 ahau	6 zoo
1764	Cabil canac	1 pop	2 - 9	⊕	3 imix	2 zoo
1765	Oxil kan	1 pop	3 - 10	⊕	4 ik	" zip
1766	Canil muluc	1 pop	4 - 11	⊕	5 akbal	" "
1767	Hoil hiix	1 pop	5 - 12	⊕	6 kan	6 zip
1768	Vacil canac	1 pop	6 = 13	⊕	7 chicchan	" zip
1769	Vucil kan	1 pop	7 = 1	⊕	8 cimi	16 voo
1770	Vaxac muluc	1 pop	8 = 2	⊕	9 manik	10 voo
1771	Bolon hiix	1 pop	9 = 3	⊕	10 lamat	6 voo
1772	Lahun canac	1 pop	10 = 4	⊕	11 muluc	7 voo
1773	Buluc kan	1 pop	11 = 5	⊕	12 oc	" pop
1774	Lahcal muluc	1 pop	12 6	⊕	13 chuen	pop.

Figure 4.3. An interweaving of calendar systems from the Códice Pérez. The right-hand column is a *tun* sequence, giving the Maya month date on which the *tun* falls (Códice Pérez ca. 1875: 72, p. 124 following Roys 1949a). Courtesy of the Princeton Collection of Western Americana, Princeton University Library.

with numbered Ahau signs in association. Based on Gann's (1900) tracings, there is a sequence of Ahau dates that fits the pattern that can only be *tun* endings (Thompson 1965: 349). Thompson (1957: 611) refers to the figures as "patrons." There is no apparent historical information on these panels, although some of the noncalendrical glyphs could be names of persons or places.

A rare hieroglyph appears in both the Paris Codex and the Santa Rita murals (Fig. 4.5), but there do not seem to be any one-to-one correspondences between the series otherwise. The Santa Rita mural figures are not seated on *tun* signs, the art style is radically different, and many of the mural figures are roped together in a chain, reminiscent more of a procession than the individually placed figures in the Paris.

Tun counts were not restricted to the Postclassic Period; the Classic Maya also recorded them. (The following interpretation is based on David Stuart, personal communication, 1989.) On the north and south sides of Stela J (Fig. 4.6) at Copan, dated 9.13.10.0.0. (A.D. 702), there is reference to the upcoming completion of the ninth *baktun* (a period of twenty *katuns*) and the beginning (A.D. 830) of the new tenth *baktun*. What follows is a count of *tuns* of which one through sixteen are legible. The text reads *hun tun i-yu-wa-la* —?—, *ka tun i-yu-wa-la* —?—, *ox tun i-yu-wa-la* —?—, etc. *Yuual,* in seventeenth-century Chontal (Smailus 1975: 179), is a term meaning "then" or "in order" and is used to introduce "subordinate clauses." The subordinate clauses on the Copan stela are not understood at this time, but they are glyph groups found to be associated with numbered *tuns* on other monuments as well. So the translation reads "one *tun* in order —?—, two *tuns* in order —?—, three *tuns* in order —?—," etc. The important point for this discussion is that the Maya saw fit to re-

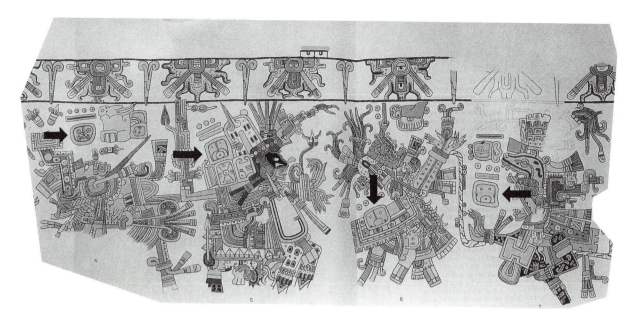

Figure 4.4. A *tun* sequence from the Santa Rita murals, reading from right to left, 8 Ahau, 4 Ahau, 13 Ahau, 9 Ahau (Gann 1900 : Plate 29).

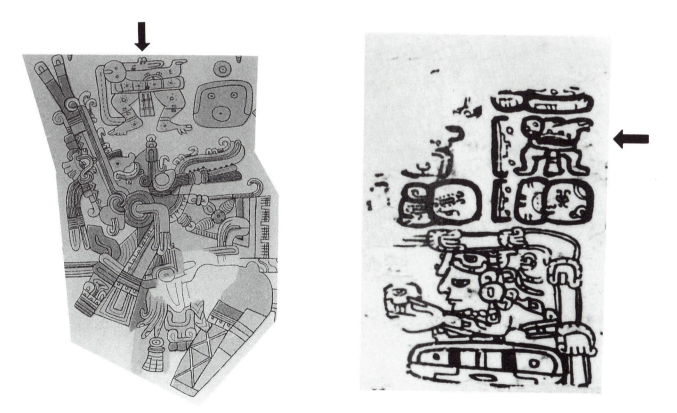

Figure 4.5. Parallel glyphs from, *left,* Santa Rita (Gann 1900 : Plate 29) and, *right,* Paris, page 5. Paris Codex courtesy of Phot. Bibl. Nat. Paris.

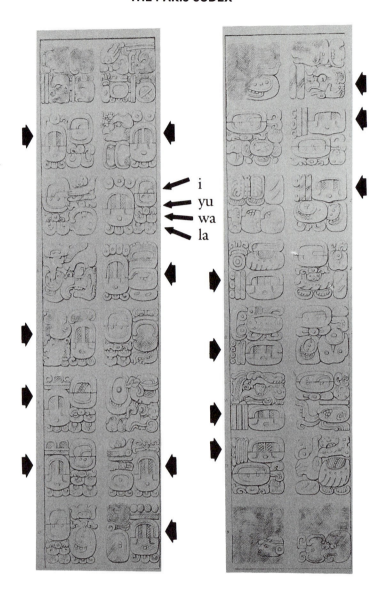

i
yu
wa
la

Figure 4.6. Tun count on Copan Stela J; from *top left*, 1 *tun*, to *bottom right*, 16 *tun*(Maudslay 1889–1902: vol. 1, Plate 69). *I-yu-wa-la*, or *yuual*, means "then" or "in order" (D. Stuart, personal communication 1989).

cord a series of *tuns* that lay in the future, the first *tuns* of the upcoming new *baktun*. This suggests that Maya were recording prophecy, not writing about past historical events.

To summarize how the Maya used *tun* counts in the Colonial and pre-Hispanic eras, counts of *tuns* sometimes had historical content but just as often functioned more in the context of prophecy and omen-reading. Marking the passage of *tuns* was important, but the function of such counts in Maya society remains elusive. Numbered *tuns*

very likely had their own omens which colored predictions and prognostications for upcoming events.

READING THE *TUN* SEQUENCE

In the case of the Paris Codex, it is apparent from the illustrations on the *tun* signs that a series of omens has been set out with which the priest could give his readings. Unfortunately, the destruction of most of the hieroglyphic texts makes it difficult to confirm this, but a comparison with the yearbearer pages supports this notion. Based on the predominance of the Corn God in these scenes, the interpretations probably deal with maize crops. If the purpose of the pages was to give omens for the *tuns,* the figures seated on the *tun* signs would be read by the priests much like the images on the yearbearer pages on the reverse side of the codex—as general fates for the associated periods. In the case of the yearbearers, the periods are 365-day years; in the case of the *tun* pages, the periods are 360 days.

If the reading of omens was the function of these pages, the actual mechanics of the sequence is still to be discussed. It is fairly certain there were once thirteen pages here, as explained above. There are three *tun* signs with figures on each page, with the possibility of a fourth sign on some pages. In the space between the signs, there are two Ahau dates. Reading across the bottom Ahaus, one finds a *tun* sequence from 3 Ahau to 2 Ahau; reading only the top signs and again moving across from page to page, one finds another *tun* sequence reaching from 9 Ahau to 8 Ahau (Fig. 4.1). These sequences were longer in the original when all thirteen pages were intact. The question remains, which *tun* series was read in what order, and which omen was read for which date?

There is one intriguing clue in the *tun* illustration on page 8. In the far right picture, there is a *uinic* and a *tun* sign (Fig. 4.7). The *uinic* sign is used for the number twenty in the God C pages on the other side of the codex (see below). If, for the sake of argument, the *tun* count started on page 2 (the first legible page of the present codex), and the calendar priest counted across thirteen pages, he would come back to page 2 again for the fourteenth *tun* and keep counting up to twenty. The twentieth *tun* of his count would fall on the page with the *uinic-tun* sign, a sign meaning twenty *tuns.* If the Ah Kin was counting the top row of Ahaus, his count would end on 11 Ahau, whereas counting the bottom row would take him to 5 Ahau. These dates, depending on which row he was counting, mark the last day of the last *tun* in a twenty-*tun* series. As twenty *tuns* make one *katun,* they would also represent the last day of the *katun* within which

the twenty *tuns* were counted. The top row, starting on page 2 of the codex, represents the twenty *tuns* in *katun* 11 Ahau, and the bottom row can be used to count the twenty *tuns* of *katun* 5 Ahau.

If the end of *katun* 3 Ahau was approaching and the priest wanted to know the omens for the twenty *tuns* in the upcoming *katun,* he could enter the table at 3 Ahau, the last day of *katun* 3 Ahau, and then count twenty *tuns* forward from that point. It is still not clear which of the three illustrations on each page he used to read his omens; he may have used all three at once; or perhaps he used the middle pictures for counting the first thirteen *tuns* and then doubled back to the beginning to finish the count from fourteen to twenty, using the right-hand pictures to avoid repetition. We know the Maya were skilled at reading more than one omen for any particular period.

UINAL COUNTS

Why are there two rows of Ahau dates when only one is needed to record a sequence of *tuns*? Again, the Chilam Balams provide important clues. Each top Ahau sign has a number six greater than the bottom sign; for example, on page 5 the top sign is 10 Ahau and the bottom sign is 4 Ahau (Fig. 4.5, right). If read from top to bottom, this is a *uinal* interval. *Uinals,* as mentioned, are twenty-day periods. Due to the mathematics of the repeating numbers 1–13 that accompany the days, a *uinal* ending on 10 Ahau is followed by a *uinal* ending on 4 Ahau twenty days later. In the Chilam Balams of Maní and Ixil, in sections that are included in the Códice Pérez, there are counts dealing with just such sequences.

When one reviews the Chilam Balams, it becomes clear that the Colonial Maya gave great importance to recording *uinal* numbers. Pío Pérez copied a table of 260 numbers that he found on the inside cover of the original Maní manuscript (Fig. 4.8). His explanation in part reads as follows: "The following table is formed in order to count and to know the number with which ought to be designated the beginnings of each Indian month. It is known to have been arranged following the method that establishes the *Buk xok* of the

Figure 4.7. The twentieth *tun* of *katun* 11 Ahau. The *uinic-tun* sign may mean twenty *tuns*. Courtesy of Phot. Bibl. Nat. Paris.

ancient Indians" (author's translation; cf. Craine and Reindorp 1979:180; Solís Alcalá 1949:346). Pérez goes on to explain how the table works (omitted from Craine and Reindorp). If, for example, a year begins on 1 Kan, one finds the number 1 in the first line, in this case at the top left-hand corner of the table. Reading across horizontally, one sees the number 8. This signifies that the second month of the year will begin on 8 Kan, the third will be 2 Kan, and so on. According to Pérez's explanation, the original table was more complex, including columns of day signs beside the vertical number columns and incorporating ways of moving diagonally to the right and left within the table to find the proper sequences of coefficients.

A simpler table (Fig. 4.9) exists in the Maní proper (Códice Pérez ca. 1875:105; Craine and Reindorp 1979:177; Solís Alcalá 1949:340–341). It reads:

one to eight
eight to two
two to nine
nine to three

three to ten
ten to four
four to eleven
eleven to five
five to twelve
twelve to six
six to thirteen
thirteen to seven
seven to one
one to eight
eight to two
two to nine
nine to three
three to ten
ten to four Muluc, 1st of Pop.

The explanation beside this table says in part: ". . . 5 Kan is the first day of Pop, and the sequence of the months begins where its says 'four passes to eleven,' as is arranged in the table to the left." Although there are many calendrical errors and miscounts in the Colonial manuscripts, the point here is the apparent survival from earlier sources of a simple table by which, no matter what day the first of Pop falls on, the first day of

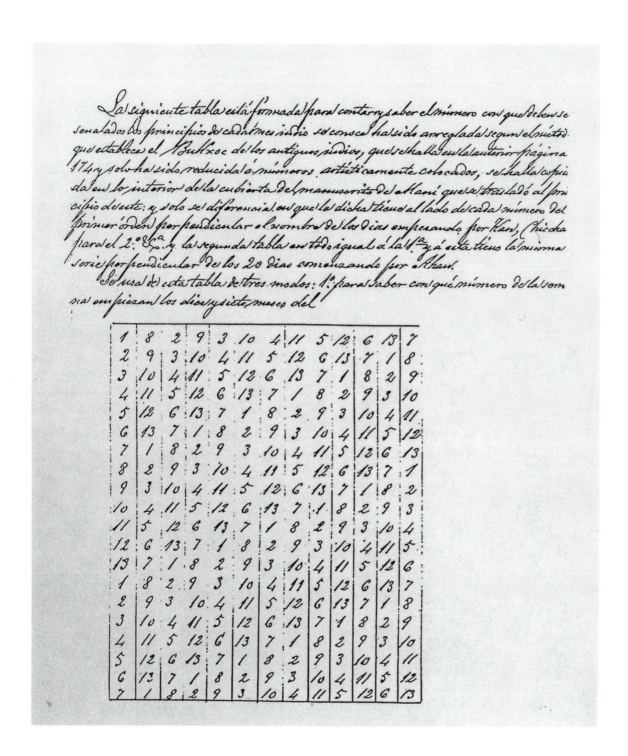

Figure 4.8. Table from Códice Pérez used for tabulating beginning dates of succeeding *uinals* (Códice Pérez ca 1875:105). Courtesy of the Princeton Collection of Western Americana, Princeton University Library.

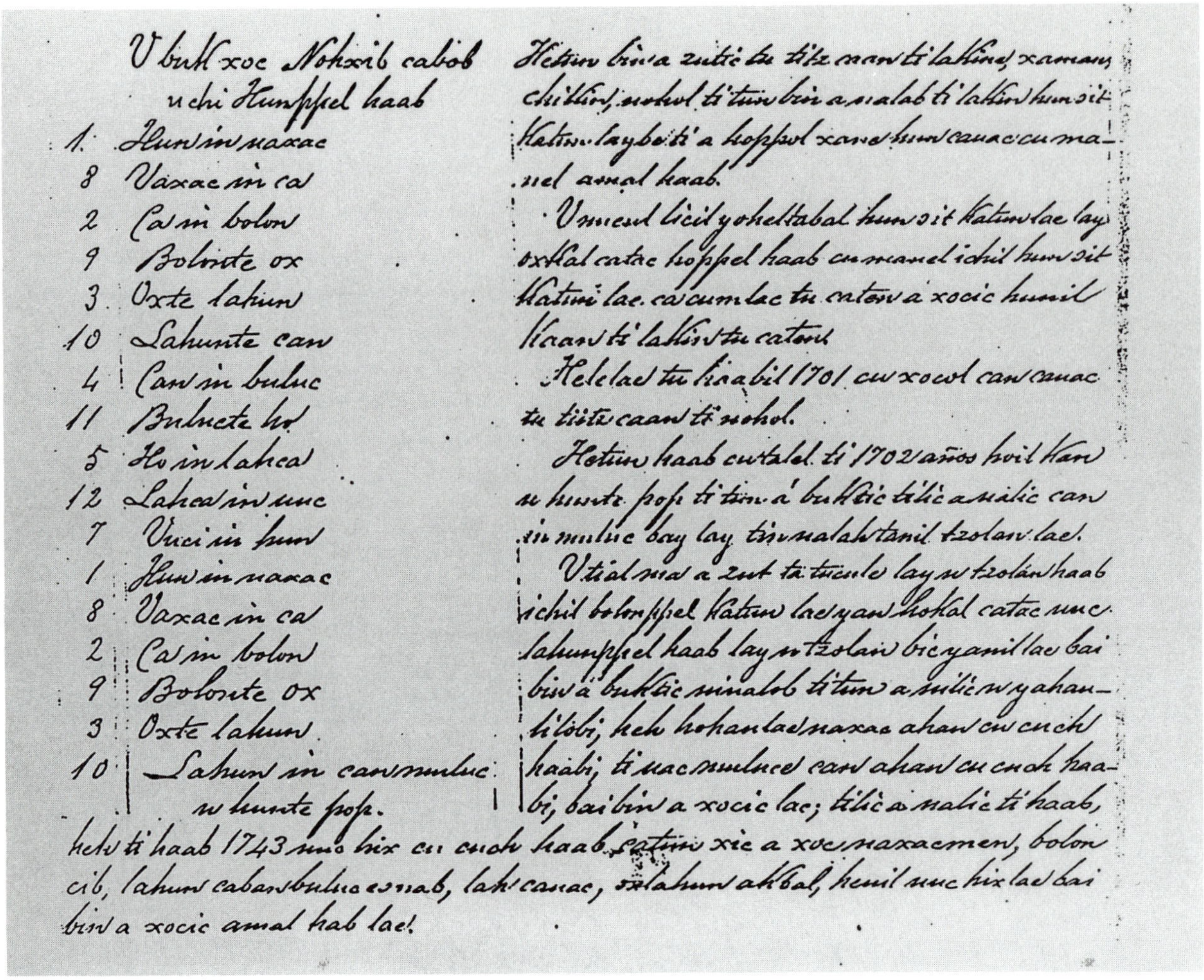
U buk xoc Nohxib cabob
u chi Hunppel haab
1. Hun in uaxac
8 Uaxac in ca
2 Ca in bolon
9 Bolonte ox
3. Oxte lahun
10 Lahunte can
4 Can in buluc
11 Buluctè ho
5 Ho in lahca
12 Lahca in uuc
7 Uuci in hun
1 Hun in uaxac
8 Uaxac in ca
2 Ca in bolon
9 Bolonte ox
3 Oxte lahun.
10 Lahun in can u buluc
u hunte pop.

Figure 4.9. A table for calculating *uinal* coefficients from the Chilam Balam of Maní (Códice Pérez ca. 1875:105). Courtesy of the Princeton Collection of Western Americana, Princeton University Library.

the second month is also recorded.

A further example, also from Pérez, lies in the series discussed above dealing with *tun* counts (Fig. 4.3). First the European year is given, then the yearbearer is followed by 1 Pop, then there is a double column with *uinal* counts giving the coefficient for the first day of the first two *uinals;* 9 to 3 for 1758, 10 to 4 for 1759, 11 to 5 for 1760, and so on. Month positions for *tuns* falling within these years lie at the end of each line. This particular table is especially important for understanding the Ahau dates in the Paris Codex. In the Maní example, discussed above (Fig. 4.9), even though the *uinal* numbers are arranged in a column only two numbers wide, the whole makes a continuous count: 1 to 8, 8 to 2, and so forth. They are successive *uinals.* In the Códice Pérez example (Fig. 4.3), the *uinal* numbers are not successive *uinals,* but only the first two *uinals* of successive years. The Maya scribe gave the *uinal* numbers for the first and second month of particular years.

As one can see from this perusal of the Chilam Balams, a 260-day table copied by Pérez was expressly used to determine *uinal* numbers. A *uinal* count was arranged in a vertical column two numbers wide with an explanation that, whatever day a year started on, the table could be used to find the last day of the first and second *uinals* of that year. Another *uinal* count, also only two numbers wide, was embedded in a list of years, yearbearers, and *tun* ending dates, not forming a continuous *uinal* count but clearly marking only the first two *uinal* coefficients for any particular year. When one applies these Colonial Period models to the pre-Hispanic Paris Codex, the double set of Ahau numbers found between the *tun* figures is explained.

Given any *tun* ending date, the priest could locate that date in the upper Ahau numbers of the Paris *tun* pages. The Ahau date directly below it is the day exactly one *uinal* later. If the pairs of Ahau numbers on these pages were arranged vertically, they would produce a double row of numbers very similar to the *uinal* columns in the Chilam Balams. Beginning on page 2, they would read 13 to 7, 9 to 3, 5 to 12 (visible on page 4), 1 to 8, and so on. It is far from clear just why such a count was important to the Maya, especially when it is so easy to figure *uinal* days mentally,

without writing them down, but the evidence from the Chilam Balams makes it clear that just such a count was full of meaning to the ritual practitioners of the past.

SUMMARY

The upper register of the *katun* pages deals with *tuns* and *uinals*. Read horizontally, a *tun* sequence of Ahau dates runs across the pages, accompanied by omens on *tun* signs, mostly dealing with maize. Coupled with the *tun* count is a *uinal* count of a type that survived into the Colonial Chilam Balams, a count in which, given any date, the number for the date one *uinal* later is given. This *uinal* count is recorded in the vertical columns of two Ahau dates on each page, read from top to bottom, one column at a time. The omens on these pages were integrated by the working priest into readings for *tuns* within *katuns* and *uinals* within *tuns*.

5

God C Pages

God C was given his name by Paul Schellhas (1904). Taube (1992) provides a more recent treatment of God C, showing the great antiquity of this god, who goes back at least to the Maya proto-Classic. Schellhas and others have noted how elusive God C is to identify. His glyph is ubiquitous in the inscriptions, but his identity and function are not clear. Recently, epigraphers have begun to read the glyph as Ku (Ringle 1988; Carlson 1989), a generic term in Yucatec Mayan for "god." The reason he has never been precisely identified is because Ku does not refer to a specific god. He is used generically, as in the expressions *bolon ti ku* "nine god" or *ku na* "god house" (temple or church). In this chapter, his interchangeability with the rain god Chac is demonstrated.

CONTENTS

The God C pages fill the top two-thirds of pages 15–18 in the Paris Codex. The upper and lower divisions are set off by thick red lines. The bottom third of these pages are almanacs (described in Chapter 6). The pages are divided into *t'ols,* a term from the Vienna Dictionary (Mengin 1972: 42r) used by Thompson (1972:19), meaning "a column of a book." They are like standard almanacs from the other codices, but here each *t'ol* has a vertical column of bars and dots preceding it. God C, in various attitudes and locations, dominates both the scenes and the hieroglyphic texts.

ILLUSTRATIONS

The key to understanding the God C pages in the Paris Codex lies in a comparison with the Chac pages in the Dresden Codex; there are many

points of similarity in the two. The first correspondence to be explored is the relationship of God C and Chac.

In the Paris, the illustrations show Ku in many places, be it temple, platform, or tree, and he is holding something or doing something in each scene. In one of the *t'ols* he is replaced by a Chac, in another by a Pauahtun, suggesting an interchangeability of these spirit concepts. Most every scene has either a direct counterpart or a close resemblance to a corresponding scene in the Dresden Chac pages.

In Figure 5.1, the Paris God C scenes are presented in order and the analogous Dresden scenes are given. The action of the players, their ritual garb and religious paraphernalia, their postures and positions, and their offerings find manifestation in these two sacred books in such likeness that it can only reflect a common intellectual underlayer. The scenes are different—certainly one was not copied from the other—but they are close enough in meaning to reveal their common source, a shared Maya belief system in which Chac and God C are almost interchangeable.

PARALLEL TEXTS

Similarities between the Paris and Dresden codices are also reflected linguistically. The hieroglyphic texts in the Paris God C pages and four almanacs in the Dresden Chac pages share an almost identical initial verb, probably *aan* "to be (in a place)" (Fox and Justeson 1984:56–58). The main sign of the initial compound is the same, despite different sets of affixes (Figs. 5.2, 5.3).

The second sign in each Paris text is Ku "god," producing the opening phrase "There is

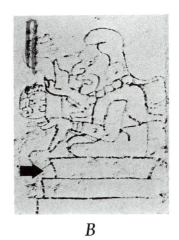

A   B

T'ol 1   *A,* Paris page 15, top left, mostly erased; edge of temple visible. *B,* Dresden 42a, a similar stepped platform.

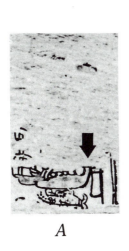

A   B

T'ol 2   *A,* Diving figure as in *t'ol* 20 with arm visible holding a maize tamale. Under his arm is a difficult-to-identify icon, possibly the sea creature with the split tail seen in the constellation page. *B,* Dresden 41c, a diving Chac but not in a temple. Note necklace beads resting on his arm in both pictures.

T'ol 3   Erased.

Figure 5.1. A comparison of the Paris God C pages, *t'ol* 1–24, and corresponding scenes in the Dresden Codex Chac pages. Paris Codex courtesy of Phot. Bibl. Nat. Paris; Dresden Codex courtesy of American Philosophical Society.

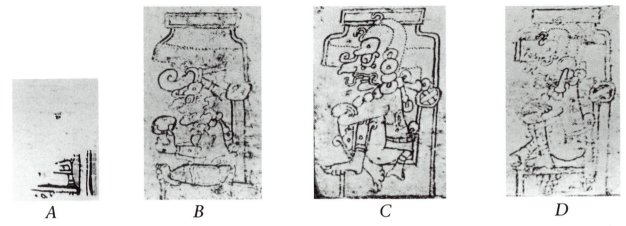

T'ol 4 *A,* Paris page 16, top left, God seated in a temple structure; cf. Paris 18a. *B, C,* and *D,* Dresden 33c, 35c, and 38c, similar temples with seated Chacs.

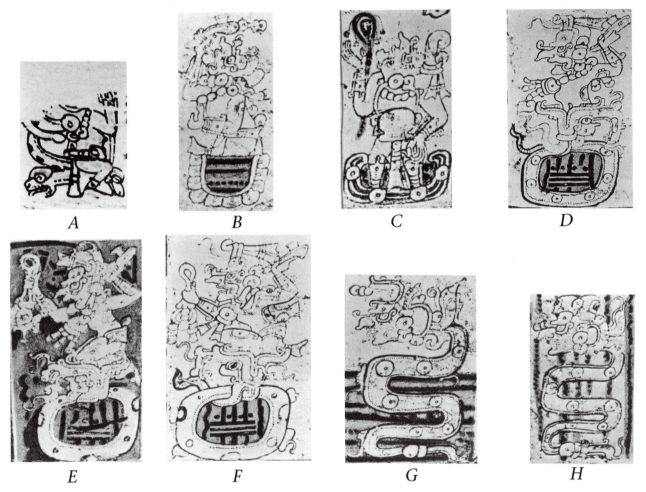

T'ol 5 *A,* God C with two snakes coiling around him, head thrown back, arm up. *B* and *C,* Dresden 34c and 36c, Chac with head thrown back, arm up. *D, E,* and *F,* Dresden 33b, 34b, and 35b, Chac appears in the jaws of snakes with water markings encircling rainfall. *G* and *H,* Dresden 35b and 36a, shown in water; there are snakes with Chac heads and water markings. *Canil ha* is snake of the water or water snake; *caanil ha* is sky of the water or rain. The scene here in the Dresden is a Maya wordplay for rain. *Caanil chac* also means rain in Yucatec, a "reading" for the snakes with Chac heads.

T'ol **6**   Erased.

T'ol **7**   Paris page 17, top left, feet and legs visible on some kind of platform or structure with unidentified mammal. No Dresden counterpart.

A B

T'ol **8**   *A,* Temple with a burning spiked brazier in front, as in Dresden New Year page 26b. *B,* Dresden 40c, Chac with incense burner, unspiked variety.

T'ol **9**   Erased.

A B C

T'ol **10**   *A,* Paris page 18, top left, God in temple. *B,* and *C,* Dresden 33c and 35c, Chacs in temples.

A   *B*

T'ol **11**   *A,* God piercing his penis, blood streaming out. *B,* Dresden 37b, Chac holding his penis with some kind of flow coming out, ending in a bird head.

T'ol **12**   Erased.

T'ol **13**   Paris page 15, center left, erased.

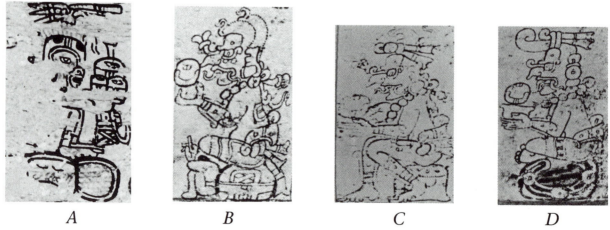

A   *B*   *C*   *D*

T'ol **14**   *A,* Seated *Ku* with stacked tamales. *B, C,* and *D,* Dresden 35c, 38a, and 39c, Chacs holding tamales.

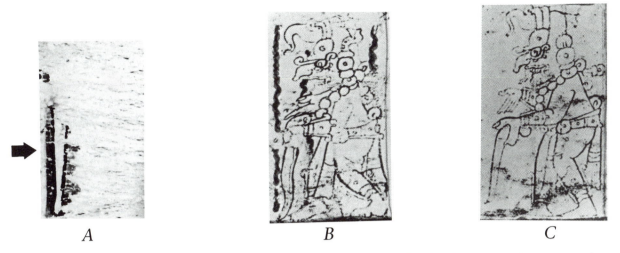

T'ol 15   *A,* Probably a planting stick. *B* and *C,* Dresden 38b and 39b, Chacs with planting sticks.

T'ol 16   *A,* Paris page 16, center left, *Ku* seated in unidentified plant emerging from a waterhole (pond?, cenote?). *B, C, D, E, F,* and *G,* Dresden 29c, 33a, 36c, 38c, 39c and 43a, similar water features.

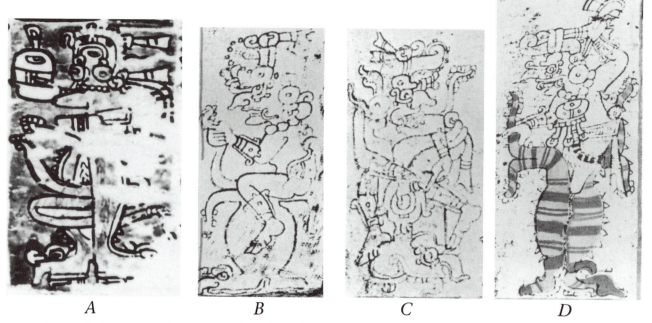

A *B* *C* *D*

T'ol 17 *A, Ku* in a ceiba tree. *B, C,* and *D,* Dresden 40a, 67c, and 69a, Chacs in ceiba trees; note the snake-head roots and distinguishing flowers.

T'ol 18 Erased.

T'ol 19 *A,* Paris page 17, center left, *Ku* seated on a snake draped over a spiked censer. No direct Dresden counterpart.

A *B*

T'ol 20 *A,* A descending Chac in a temple holding a maize tamale. *B,* Dresden 41c, a descending Chac.

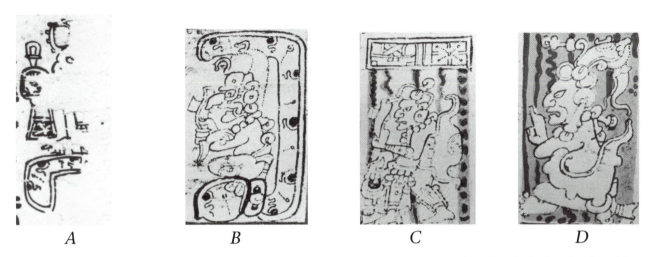

T'ol **21**   *A,* A Pauahtun seated on a cave symbol holding a tamale with a ritual cloth. The headdress is the distinguishing mark (cf. Pauahtun figures at the top of Paris 22). *B,* Dresden 30a, Chac in a cave. *C* and *D,* Dresden 37a and 41b, Pauahtuns.

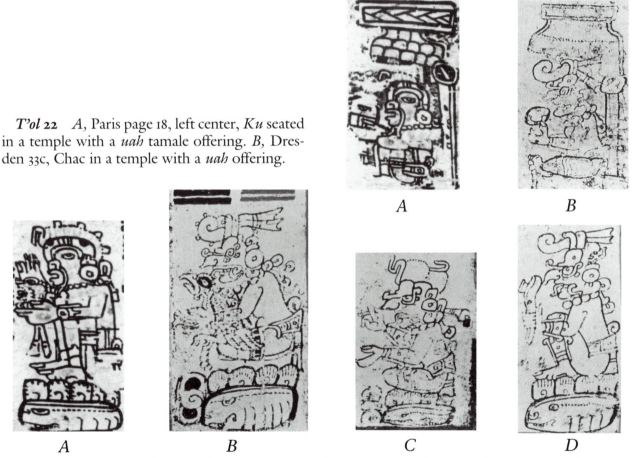

T'ol **22**   *A,* Paris page 18, left center, *Ku* seated in a temple with a *uah* tamale offering. *B,* Dresden 33c, Chac in a temple with a *uah* offering.

T'ol **23**   *A, Ku* seated on unidentified signs, holding a fishlike offering with scales and a forked tail. *B, C,* and *D,* Dresden 69b, 37c, and 40a, Chacs seated on the same signs but without the fish offering.

T'ol **24**   Erased.

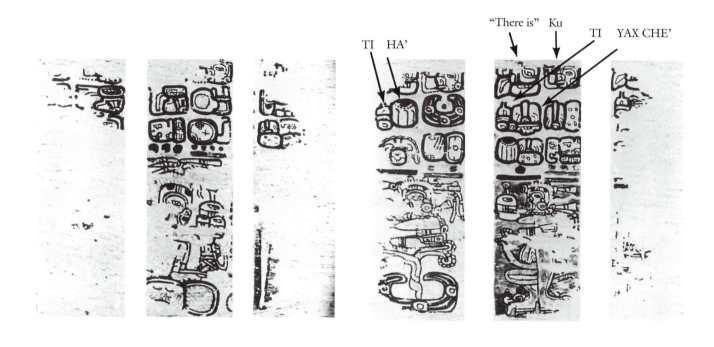

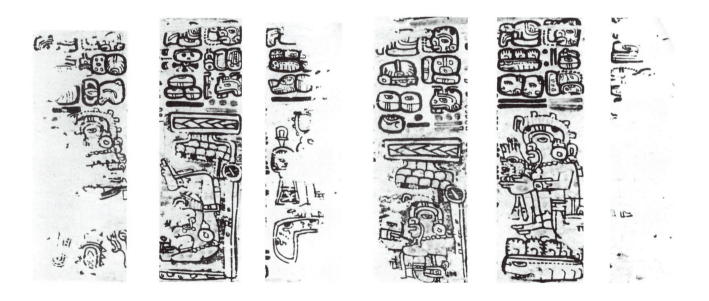

Figure 5.2. Glyphs and pictures from God C pages, reading from top left to bottom right, *t'ols* 13–24. Each *t'ol* begins with "there is," the same format as in some Dresden Chac almanacs (cf. Fig. 5.3). Courtesy of Phot. Bibl. Nat. Paris.

Figure 5.3. Dresden Chac almanacs, reading from top left to bottom right, pages 30–39. Most *t'ols* begin with "there is Chac." The first glyph compound has the same main sign as the Paris pages (cf. Fig. 5.2). Courtesy of American Philosophical Society.

Ku" (Fig. 5.2). One of the Chac almanacs in the Dresden Codex shares this same syntactic structure of verb and subject, placing the name of the god in the second position (Fig. 5.3). The Paris almanacs start "There is Ku," while the corresponding Dresden piece begins "There is Chac."

In the Paris series, the location of Ku is generally written in the second line of text. The clue is the *ti* "at" glyph, even if the reading of where he is "at" is not clear. On page 16 there is *ti ha (?)* "at the water" and *ti yaxche* "at the ceiba tree" (Fig. 5.2). On page 18 an undeciphered sign appears in the second row of text without the locative *ti,* but there is no doubt it spells the place in question because the same glyphs are found under the seated Ku in the picture.

GOD C PAGES AS ALMANACS

If the vertical rows of bars and dots are eliminated on these pages, as in Figure 5.2, what is left has the appearance of a standard set of one or more almanacs with all the basic elements of almanac formation, *except* there is no visible column of day signs marking the beginning (see Chapter 6). If there is a missing column of day signs, it must have been on a missing page; the erased left edge of page 15 must have contained a vertical numbers column like the other *t'ols,* so it could not have been there. The missing day-sign column is one argument for there being at least one missing page preceding page 15.

Each *t'ol* has a set of six glyph blocks with parallel syntax and a picture illustrating the information given in the glyphs. Between the glyphs and the pictures, just as in the Dresden almanacs, are black and red numbers, the black being the intervals, or distance numbers, and the red being the day reached for that particular *t'ol.* The series across the center section can be reconstructed; the top section is gone.

Gates (1910) reconstructed the red and black numbers in the middle section, offering two alternative readings that differ only slightly. His first reading appears to be the correct one. The numerical total, adding the reconstructed black distance numbers, is 82, with missing unrecoverable numbers at both ends of the series. This number, 82, provides important evidence; to wit, this almanac cannot be a typical 260-day variety

because in 260-day almanacs the distance numbers across a set of *t'ols* typically add up to 26 (10 × 26 = 260), 52 (5 × 52 = 260), or 65 (4 × 65 = 260).

If the Ku almanacs are indeed almanacs beginning with a column of day names (now missing), the smallest possible division that can incorporate 82 plus days is 104. There is such an almanac in the Chac pages of the Dresden Codex (35b–41b), being a "double almanac" of 520 days with five divisions of 104 days each. Another Chac almanac (Dresden 30c–33c) has nine *t'ols* adding up to 117 days, repeated twenty times. Hence, the extra long intervals in the Paris Ku pages find their counterparts in the Dresden Chac pages, further reinforcing the general correspondences between the two.

NUMBER COLUMNS

The vertical rows of bar-and-dot numbers between the Ku pictures have puzzled students of this codex for years (Fig. 5.4). One explanation is that of Ernst Förstemann: "In the Peresianus . . . the numbers are mixed up in a senseless fashion, as if to tempt the reader to seek in them for a meaning which is not at all present" (Förstemann 1903:25). In spite of his contention that the numbers are meaningless, Förstemann did discover one repeating set of numbers—perhaps an important clue. A series of black numbers, 3, 6, 16, 19, 4, appears on page 16 and again on 18 and *maybe* on 15.

To think that the numbers represent artistic expression without specific meaning would be, as William Gates has said, "a mere begging of the question" (1910:26). Gates, in fact, expended great energy on the numbers series while investigating the colors of the codex in general because he felt the solution to the bar-and-dot riddle depended absolutely on determining their separation, one from another, accomplished in Maya fashion by alternating colors. To the best of Gates's research, using three facsimiles and a detailed questionnaire sent to the National Library in Paris, he securely identified three separate colors in the number columns—red, black, and blue-green—with perhaps a fourth, brown. In spite of this, he could not resolve the meaning of the signs.

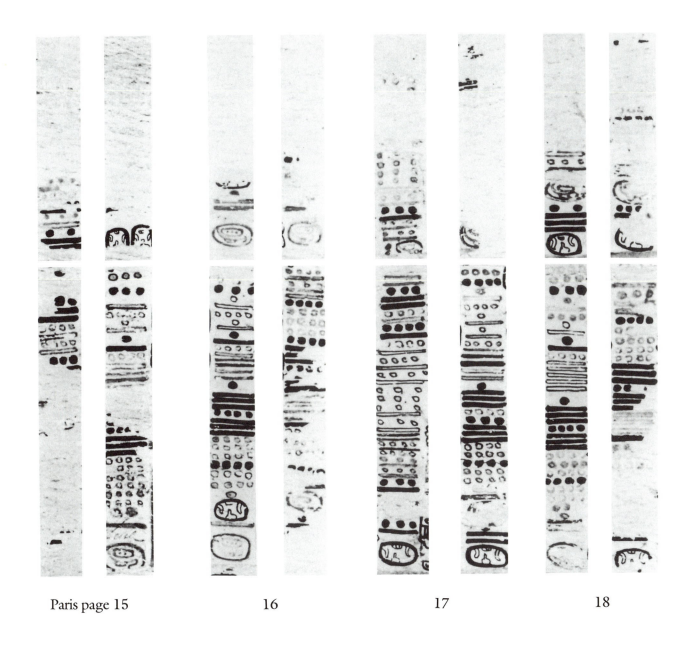

Paris page 15   16   17   18

Red *kal* sign,
the number 20

Black *uinic* sign,
the number 20

Figure 5.4. The number columns from the Paris God C pages, upper and lower divisions. Courtesy of Phot. Bibl. Nat. Paris.

Figure 5.5. Signs for "twenty" in a Dresden Chac almanac, pages D40c–41c. Courtesy of American Philosophical Society.

Kal Numbers

At the bottom of each column is a red sign for "twenty" with at least one red bar over it (Fig. 5.4). Again, a clue to the meaning is found in the Dresden Chac pages, in this case, the almanac across the bottom of pages 40–41 (Fig. 5.5). In each of the six *t'ols* in this otherwise common-variety almanac, a number is incorporated in the scene below; in all cases the number uses the sign for "twenty," *kal* in Yucatec, sometimes by itself, sometimes with bars and dots. Thompson (1972), following Förstemann (1906), reads these, one for each *t'ol,* as 26, 20, 39 (split by the skyband), 26, 39, and 26 and suggests the 20 is a mistake because it alone is not a multiple of 13. There is a better interpretation.

The solution to this riddle lies in the Dresden New Year pages, where there are similar black numbers with the sign *kal* "twenty," with the glyph *tu* attached (Fig. 5.6). In the bottom sections of the four New Year pages (25c–28c), these numbers are found in scenes where priests dressed as gods are tossing incense (Love 1986: 184, 190; 1987). Braziers are shown on pages 25 and 26, but are suppressed on 27 and 28. On pages 26c–28c, the sign for the number twenty,

with bars and dots, floats in space, as it were, but on page 25c, the corresponding black number, this time the number nineteen, sits in the mouth of a ceramic incense burner. The Maya artist used this pictorial device to show what was in the brazier; in other words, "nineteen incense," probably pellets or balls of incense, were in the incense burner. On the following pages, the pictures show the priests casting the pellets, but the numbers are set above, *bolon tu kal* (29), *uac lahun tu kal* (36), *ho lahun tu kal* (35).

As an interesting aside, there has been a mild controversy, discussed by Tozzer (1921 : 101–103), over the Yucatec Maya use of the phrase *tu kal,* something like "at twenty." The debate concerns numbers greater than twenty, such as *ka tu ox kal,* which could be read "two *in* the third twenty" (42) or "two *and* three twenties" (62). Beltran (1746) gives a mixed system, Thomas (1897–1898: 891–893) opts for the latter, and Pío Pérez (1898: 119) is ambiguous, giving *ox lahun tu kal* as 33 (13 and 20) but *ox lahun tu ox kal* as 53 (13 in the third 20). Happily, there is agreement when only one *kal* is involved. *Buluc tu kal* would be 31 in all sources, even though the system gets mixed for higher numbers. Readings for the numbers in the Dresden New Year pages are therefore secure:

Figure 5.6. Signs for "twenty" in the Dresden New Year pages (D25c–28c). Courtesy of American Philosophical Society.

Page 25	bolon lahun	nineteen
Page 26	bolon tu kal	twenty-nine
Page 27	uac lahun tu kal	thirty-six
Page 28	ho lahun tu kal	thirty-five

Based on two lines of evidence, from the Dresden Codex and from Landa, the Maya regarded offering counts as crucial to proper ritual performance. In the hieroglyphic texts at the top of the Dresden New Year pages, counts of *pom* and *ch'ahalte,* two kinds of incense, are recorded (Love 1987). The *pom* counts on respective pages are 9, 7, 11, and 6; for *ch'ahalte,* 7, 16, 5, and 6. From this textual evidence alone it is clear that very specific numbers were assigned to ritual offerings. Strong support comes from Landa's description of New Year ceremonies; in one ceremony the priest incensed the image of Kan u Uayeyab, an idol, with "forty-nine grains of maize ground up with their incense" (Tozzer 1941:140), and in another year, Chac u Uayeyab was "perfumed with fifty-three grains of ground maize

with their incense" (ibid.:144). During other parts of the ceremony, when the priests were on the road from the edge of town to the center, they were given special drinks, in one case made with 415 grains of parched maize (ibid.:141), in another year with 380 grains (ibid.:144).

Although the meaning of these numbers escapes the modern student, the point is clear that very precise counts of ingredients were essential to correct ritual performance. This explains the black numbers in the Dresden Chac pages (Fig. 5.5). In the Chac almanac, just as in the New Year pages, the numbers specify offering quantities for the rites performed; in the case of the Chacs, they are rituals at the stations of the 260-day almanac.

The Dresden Chac numbers do not have the *tu* sign found in the New Year pages. Without the *tu,* the bar-and-dot numbers become multipliers recording counts of twenties. In other words, *ox lahun tu kal* is read 13 and 20, or 33, but *ox lahun kal* reads thirteen twenties, or 260. Reading the Chac numbers in this way gives the following:

Figure 5.7. Offering counts using the *uinic* "twenty" sign in the Dresden New Year pages, D25–28. Courtesy of American Philosophical Society.

Page 40c, *t'ol* 1	uac kal	120	
Page 40c, *t'ol* 2	kal	20	
Page 40c, *t'ol* 3	bolon lahun kal	380	
Page 41c, *t'ol* 1	uac kal	120	
Page 41c, *t'ol* 2	bolon lahun kal	380	
Page 41c, *t'ol* 3	uac kal	120	

It is interesting that 380, appearing twice, is the number given by Landa for one of the above-mentioned ritual drinks, made of 380 grains of parched maize.

With these comparisons in mind, it becomes a reasonable hypothesis that the red *kal* numbers in the Paris number columns serve the same purpose, prescribing correct sums for ritual ingredients. Further support follows:

Uinic Numbers

Along with the red *kal* numbers at the base of the Paris number columns, there are in some cases black *uinic* signs, with or without bars and dots (Fig. 5.4). These too probably represent counts of offerings. In the Dresden New Year pages *uinic* signs with bars and dots occur in all the top scenes in which the opossum actors are walking, carrying the idols for the *uayeb* ceremonies (Fig. 5.7). In Landa, as already mentioned, special drinks are given to priests during processions from the edge of town to the center—drinks containing 415 and 380 grains of parched maize for

the Kan years and the Muluc years, respectively. The same drink is provided for the priests in the other years, but the numbers are not given. The *uinic* signs in the Dresden scenes, being numbers, probably refer to this or something quite similar. The two places where Landa gives exact counts of offerings or ingredients are the same two places where counts are given in the Dresden New Year pages, when the priest is walking to town and when the incensing is performed in front of the *uayeyab* standard.

Each *uinic* sign stands for twenty, based on the sign's use for the *uinal* twenty-day period and the use of *uinic* and its cognates in several Mayan languages for "man" and "twenty" (Thompson 1950:143–144). On Dresden 26a, three *uinic* signs and a bar-and-dot thirteen add up to seventy-three; page 27 has sixty-two, page 28 has seventy-three again. Page 25, however, is a bit problematical because there are two bar-and-dot numbers, one above the *uinic* signs and the other below. A likely solution is that the eight and the three *uinics* are read together as in the other pages, here totaling sixty-eight, while the nine refers to another offering, perhaps the nine *pom* written in the hieroglyphic text above.

The argument for reading these *uinic* signs as offering counts is a little weaker than the *kal* sign offerings where the numbers are placed directly in an incense burner. The *uinic* signs are not shown in or on anything, but if the offering

HUH UAH (Iguana Tamale)

(wa)-UAH (Maize Tamale)

cu–ts(u), cuts (turkey)

Fish

Figure 5.8. Offering counts using the *uinic* "twenty" sign, Dresden 42c–45c. Courtesy of American Philosophical Society.

count hypothesis is applied to scenes elsewhere in the codices, it provides reasonable interpretations for heretofore unexplained pictures. Such pictures are found, once again, in the Dresden Chac pages.

In the Dresden Chac almanacs, immediately following the almanac with the *kal* signs (discussed above), clusters of *uinic* signs appear (Fig. 5.8), floating in space, as it were, along with pictures of offerings, including *uah* "maize tamale" in a vessel (page 42), *huh uah* "iguana tamale" (page 43), *cuts* spelled *cu-tsu* "turkey" (page 44), and fish (*cay?*) (page 44). Other offerings would be indicated by the *uinic* counts, 32 and 80 (page 42), 80 and 35 (page 43), 96 (page 44), and 57 and 80 (page 45).

Bunches of *uinic* signs also occur in the Madrid Codex, and in every case a count of offerings, or ingredients in offerings, is a simple, reasonable explanation (Fig. 5.9).

In the Paris Codex (Fig. 5.4) at the foot of each number column on the God C pages, there are *uinic* numbers and *kal* numbers. When compared with similar numbers in Dresden Chac almanacs, Dresden New Year pages, and Landa's description of New Year ceremonies, they appear to be counts for offerings. In the case of the Paris, the numbers serve as requisite offerings for rites associated with stations in an extended almanac greater than 260 days.

Bar-and-Dot Columns

What of the columns of bars and dots above the count signs? If the *uinic* and *kal* signs at the foot of the columns are offering counts, this implicitly suggests a similar explanation for what lies above. Support for this interpretation comes from outside the Maya zone, from Central Mexican (Mixtecan-Pueblan) codices. In the Fejervary-Mayer, the Cospi (Fig. 5.10), and the Laud codices there are pages with very similar columns or

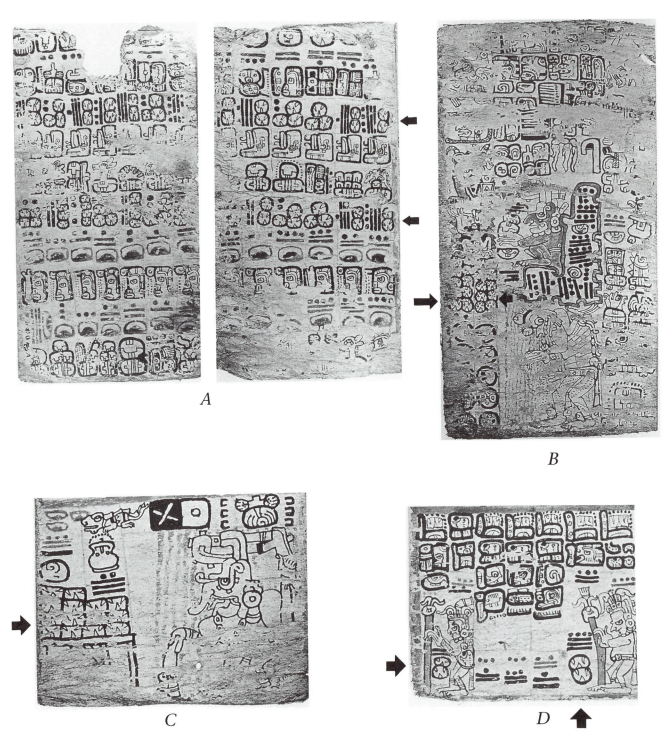

Figure 5.9. Bunches of *uinic* signs in the Madrid Codex representing counts of offerings. *A,* Madrid pages 77 and 78. *B, C,* and *D,* Madrid pages 8, 3, and 107. Courtesy of Akademische Druck- u. Verlagsanstalt.

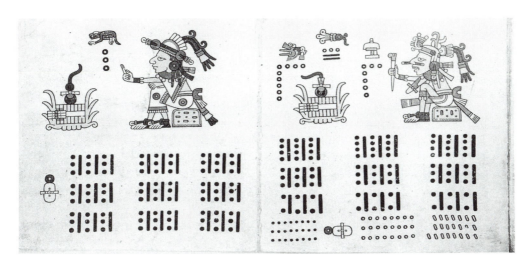

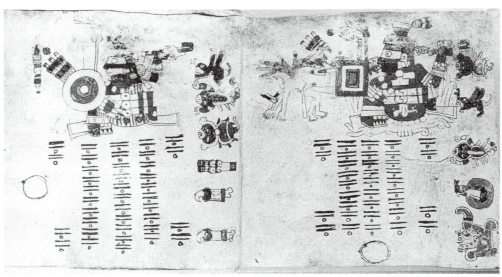

Figure 5.10. Offerings of counted bundles. *Top,* Codex Fejervary-Mayer; *bottom,* Codex Cospi. Both courtesy of Akademische Druck- u. Verlagsanstalt.

rows of Mayalike bars and dots which have been interpreted by Anton Nowotny (1961:272–274; 1968:24) as counted bundles of offerings. This interpretation is based on ethnographic fieldwork with Tlapanec Indians by Schultze Jena (1938). Nowotny writes, "Thanks to Leonhard Schultze Jena's folkloristic materials, these previously misunderstood sections can now be explained" (1961:272).

Ethnographic work by Peter van der Loo (1987) and Frank Lipp (1991) reinforce the critical role of counted bundles in modern ritual per-

formance (Fig. 5.11). Following Nowotny, van der Loo and Lipp explain the number series in the Mexican codices are pre-Columbian counterparts to modern ceremonies in which rows of bundles with specified numbers of pine needles or cane stalks are arranged near a central altar. Two examples of codex bundles, from the Fejervary-Mayer and the Cospi, are presented in Figure 5.10. It is reasonable to extend the bundle-count interpretation to the Paris Codex. Whether or not the Paris numbers represent bundles per se or other ritual objects, such as cups of sacred drink,

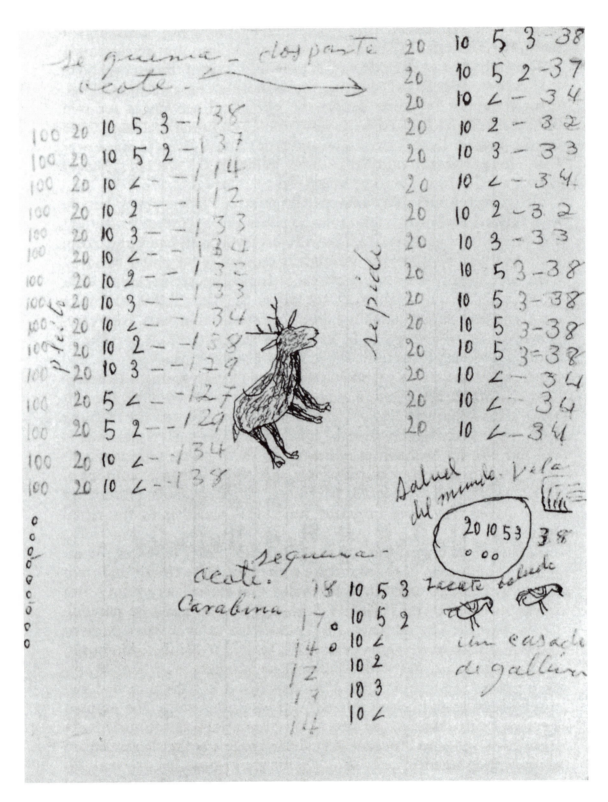

Figure 5.11. Rituals with counted bundles in modern Mixe ceremonies. From *The Mixe of Oaxaca* by Frank J. Lipp (Austin, 1991). Reprinted by permission of the University of Texas Press.

cacao beans, maize kernels, or incense balls, is not known, but the general interpretation of offerings is indicated.

If all that were present on the Paris pages were the number series without the *uinic* and *kal* signs, the offering interpretation would be only tentative, though still reasonable. Joined with the *uinic* and *kal* signs at the bottom of the columns, which are shown to be offering counts in other Maya codices, the conclusions are compelling.

SUMMARY

The God C pages are similar in many respects to the Dresden Chac pages. They contain almanacs for which the beginning pages are lost. By reading each *t'ol* in succession, horizontally, the distance numbers show that at least the lower almanac was greater than 260 days, as in some of the Chac almanacs. The God C pictures and the hieroglyphic texts share format and syntax with their Dresden counterparts. The vertical number columns between the *t'ols* represent counts of ritual offerings, recipes for proper ceremonial performances carried out at each of the stations of the almanac. Thompson has previously interpreted the Dresden almanacs as agricultural, dealing especially with weather predictions. The Paris can be likewise understood. The positions and attitudes of God C enabled the Maya priest to predict the countenances for certain days—days reached by the distance numbers above the pictures. To ensure that the gods performed as needed, the proper counts of ritual offerings were mandated.

6

Almanacs

Across the bottom of pages 15–18 (Fig. 6.1) of the Paris Codex are two or more almanacs of the variety familiar to even casual students of the codices. It is not clear who first used the term *almanac* to label these passages, which combine calendrics, illustrations, and written texts. The term comes from an Arabic word meaning "weather," or "climate." The word is appropriate to use for the Maya day counts considered here, dealing with rain and other weather phenomena.

A TYPICAL ALMANAC

Almanacs in the codices are first and foremost permutations of the 260-day *tsolkin* with several stations or resting points along its course. A *tsolkin* combines the numbers 1–13 with twenty Maya days so that the same date, e.g., 4 Ahau, repeats only every 260 days. An example from pages 13b and 14b of the Dresden Codex is illustrated (Fig. 6.2) so that one can easily see how a complete almanac works and better understand the Paris Codex example where large sections are erased.

In the example, the numerological part starts with 6 Ahau at the top of the vertical column of day signs. From there, 13, the black number to the immediate right, is added to 6 Ahau to arrive at 6 (Ben); the 6 is in red, and the day sign Ben is not shown. Continuing to the right, the black number 9 is added to arrive at red 2 (Ik), then black number 7 brings the reader to red number 9 (Muluc). Add 7, arrive at 3 (Cib), add 7, arrive at 10 (Akbal), add 9, arrive at 6 (Eb). 6 Eb, of course, is the second sign down in the vertical column of day signs at the front of the almanac. After going across the almanac horizontally adding the black numbers in succession, and having

passed through 52 days, one comes back to the next day sign down in the vertical column and again starts adding the black numbers across horizontally. Thus, after five passes of 52 days, the whole 260-day almanac is completed.

In each *t'ol* there is a picture which generally illustrates the message contained in the hieroglyphs above it. As in most almanacs, in the example used here from the Dresden Codex, the glyphs in each *t'ol* follow a parallel grammatical structure. In this case, each text of four glyph compounds begins with a verb, the action of which is illustrated in the painted scene below. The verb is followed by the object of the verb, in this case *uah*, the Yucatecan ceremonial maize tamale (Taube 1989b; Love 1989). What follows in the third glyph block is the subject—that is, the name glyph of the figure in the picture below. In the fourth block is the augury, such as good or bad, sustenance or hunger, rain or drought. The glyphs in all six *t'ols* in this example follow the same pattern: verb, object, subject, attribute. There are many variants of this pattern, but the format is usually consistent within a given almanac.

THE PARIS ALMANACS

Before studying the almanacs in the Paris, a review of the key factors in a typical almanac is helpful. The sacred round of 260 days begins with a vertical row of day names and proceeds with black and red numbers through the sequent *t'ols*; the texts of each *t'ol* follow a parallel syntactic or grammatical format; the action of the verb is illustrated in the scene below; and the subject of the text is also illustrated in the scene below.

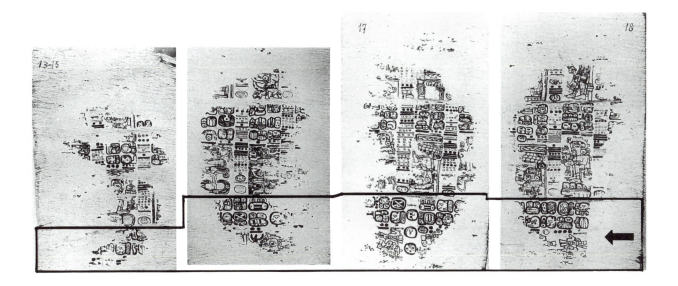

Figure 6.1. The Paris almanac section, the lower portion of the God C pages (15–18). Courtesy of Phot. Bibl. Nat. Paris.

Figure 6.2. A typical almanac from the Dresden Codex, pages 13b–14b. Courtesy of American Philosophical Society.

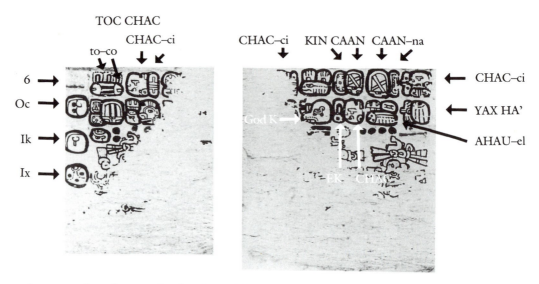

Figure 6.3. A complete 260-day almanac in the Paris Almanac, pages 17–18. Courtesy of Phot. Bibl. Nat. Paris.

Searching for these common elements in the badly damaged Paris almanacs greatly aids the analysis.

Numerology

In the four Paris pages that have almanacs, there is only one surviving vertical column of day names—on page 17 (Fig. 6.3). Visible is 6 Oc, Ik, and Ix; below Ix would be Cimi and Edznab, which have been erased. Thus there are five divisions of a 260-day round, which require in turn that the numbers reading across horizontally total 52 (52 × 5 = 260). In dealing with these numbers, the first inescapable conclusion is that there is an error near the end of this almanac on page 18. The final red 6 is correct, because the final number in all such almanacs must match the number over the vertical day-sign column at the beginning. But in working back from the final red 6, the reader finds a black 4 and a red 1, in essence reading 1 plus 4 equals 6. There is no avoiding the conclusion that either the 1 or the 4 is a mistake; either the 1 should be a 2 or the 4 should be a 5.

Gates (1910:27) and Knorozov (1982:200) have both suggested the Maya meant the final red 6 to be a 5 and that another *t'ol* with a black 1 and a red 6 was once present. A close inspection of page 18, however, reveals that the area where they have suggested the existence of another *t'ol* was always blank. There are no fragments of paint visible even where the original plaster is present.

Working back, there is a black 10 just before the red 1. From this, one can reconstruct the erased red number that just precedes the black 10. It must have been either a red 4 or 5. If the red 1 in the last *t'ol* is correct as it stands, the erased number must have been a 4; if the red 1 should have been a red 2, then the preceding red number would have been a 5 (4 + 10 = 1, or 5 + 10 = 2). It is impossible to reconstruct the erased black number from the very first column on this page. On page 17, beginning with the vertical day-sign column, the numbers of the first *t'ol* are clear: a black 22 and a red 2, producing an unmistakable sequence: 6 Oc, add 22 days and arrive at 2 Eb, with the Eb sign suppressed in typical almanac fashion. The numbers of the second *t'ol* are completely gone and unreconstructable, so the second and third *t'ols* leave a gap in the sequence. Mathematically, the black numbers from these missing *t'ols* had to have totaled either 15 or 16, again depending on the error on page 18.

On page 17, to the left of the vertical day-sign column, is the end of another almanac which also ends in a red 6, but a close examination of page 15 and 16 does not reveal where the almanac begins. It is entirely possible that the *t'ols* on pages 15, 16, and the first half of 17 are all part of the same almanac (in Dresden, pages 4–10, there is an almanac with twenty *t'ols*), but if the Paris scribe made almanacs that were similar in format to each other, one would expect another almanac of five *t'ols*, like the one on pages 17 and 18. If there was such an almanac of five *t'ols,* ending with the red 6 on page 17, the vertical day-sign column at its beginning would fall on the left margin of page 16, just preceding the "axe" glyph on that page. Instead, the remains of a glyph or glyphs are visible, indicating there was another *t'ol* there, and confirming it was not a five-*t'ol* almanac. All the visible black numbers on pages 15, 16, and the first half of 17 added together total less than 52, so the possibility remains that there is only one almanac here. One should also keep in mind that there were other pages preceding page 15, on which more almanacs or parts of almanacs may have been painted.

In summary, there is one 260-day almanac of five *t'ols* beginning with a vertical column of day signs on page 17; it is not clear whether there is more than one almanac on pages 15–17; and the almanac ending on page 17 is not a five-*t'ol* almanac.

General Subjects

It appears as though Chac, in both hieroglyphic texts and in the illustrations, is the recurring theme on these pages. There is precedent for this in the other codices, especially the Dresden, which devotes some sixteen almanacs to the Chacs. As Thompson points out (1972:94–106), these must surely be related to agriculture, especially rain. Rain, of course, is the quintessential elixir, the absolute requisite gift of nature for Maya life to endure from one harvest to the next. The unpredictable and uncertain nature of this life-giving force requires humans to prod and manipulate the spirit forces controlling it. Chacs in their several guises are supplicated by priests and lay farmers alike with prayers and offerings.

A review of the sixteenth-century Motul Dictionary (p. 290) provides some insight. (The English translations, by the author, are of the Motul glosses.)

Chac: means water in some forms of speech.
Ocol u cah Chac, the rains already came in or began.
Ocan Chac, the rains have come in or have begun.

Chelan Chac ti be yetel ichil in col, much water has fallen in the road and in my milpa.

Chaac; was a man of great stature who taught agriculture and who later became the god of breads, water, thunder and lightning; and so it is said,

Hats u cah chac, lightning strikes;
U hats chac, lightning;
Lemba u cah chac, lightning flashes;
U lemba chac, the lightning flash;
Pec u cah chac, the thunder;
Kaxal u cah chac, rain with thunder.

Reviewing these entries from the Motul Dictionary, one gets a sense of the multifaceted nature of Chac, the merging of spirit beings and natural forces.

The Texts

The almanac on pages 17 and 18 (Fig. 6.3), beginning with the vertical column of day names, has parallel syntax in its respective *t'ols.* In four of the *t'ols,* the second glyph block is visible, and in three of those, the word *chac* is present. The first *t'ol* begins *toc chac;* the second is unknown; the third ends in *chac;* the fourth is —?— *kin caan;* and the fifth is *caan* —?— *chac.*

T'ol 1, toc chac. The word *toc,* spelled *to-c(o)* in the first glyph block, is also found in the day-signs page (Chapter 8) in a picture of a rain shower, probably indicating a kind of rain. The Vienna Dictionary of Yucatec Mayan from the sixteenth or seventeenth century (Barrera Vásquez 1980:21a–25a) has the following entry: "Aguacero recio que no moja mas de la superficie de la tierra [strong rain shower that dampens no more than the surface of the land]: tocol oc haa" (Mengin 1972:7r). *Oc ha* means the rain comes or "enters." The *tocol* part of the phrase is harder to explain. *Toc* means "to burn," and in the picture below one can see the flames of a torch. In a comparable scene, in the almanac on page 16, one sees that the bearer of the torch is a vulture. Thompson (1972:54–55) refers to the Yucatec expression *kuch caan chacil* from the Chilam Balam of Chumayel (Gordon 1913:92; Roys 1933:56, 154), roughly translated "rain from a vulture sky," and he points out a vulture with rain on Dresden 38b in an almanac also dominated by the Chacs. Whatever the precise translation, *toc chac* in the Paris almanacs refers to a kind of rain, probably sudden showers called *tocol oc haa* found in the Vienna Dictionary.

T'ol 2, unknown.

T'ol 3, —?— chac. The first glyph block is gone, but the Chac glyphs in the second block are still visible.

T'ol 4, —?— kin caan. The first glyph block is undeciphered, and the second may refer to a kind of sky—in other words, weather, but *kin caan* is not a known Mayan phrase.

T'ol 5, caan —?— chac. Sky, spelled *caan-(na)*, in the first glyph block precedes the Chac spelling, but there is an unknown glyph preceding the Chac signs. *Caan chac* is often used in Maya weather terms. The Chumayel, referred to above, has a string of rain phrases, among them, *thul caan chacil, bohol caan chacil, caanil chacil,* and the aforementioned *kuch caan chacil* (Gordon 1913:92). Ethnographic investigations further reinforce the common use of this phrase. From recorded and published Maya prayers, the following examples have been extracted (Love 1986:85–86). The list reflects the original ethnographer's orthographic conventions and translations.

From Chan Kom, Yucatán (Redfield and Villa 1934):
Hatzen caan chaac "lightning sky Chac" (pp. 344, 355)
Lelen caan chaac "lightning-flash sky Chac" (pp. 344, 345, 349)
Yum bohol caan chaac "father—?—sky Chac" (pp. 345, 355)
Ttupil caan chaac "last born sky Chac" (pp. 345, 355)
Xoc tun caan chaac "count—?—sky Chac" (p. 349)

From Tusik, Quintana Roo (Villa 1945:159):
Mizen caan chaac "sweep sky Chac"
Ah thoxon caan chaac "pour-out sky Chac"
Bolon caan chaak "nine sky Chac"
Lelem caan chaak "lightning-flash sky Chac"

Hohop caan chaak "pour-from-a-vessel sky Chac"
From Santa Cruz, Quintana Roo (Gann 1918:47):
Yum caan chaacob "father sky Chacs"
From Hacienda Xcanchakan, Yucatán (Brasseur de Bourbourg 1870:102):
Ah tsolan caan chaac "arranged-in-order sky Chac"

When the Maya name a profusion of rain gods, they are also referring to the many kinds of rain that affect their daily lives, especially rains that affect the milpa. The rains are supplicated and entreated in Maya prayer. Chacs are gods that bring rain, but at the same time, *chacs are* rain.

Returning to the Paris almanac on pages 17–18 (Fig. 6.3) and the discussion of parallel syntactic structure, we have now seen that the top two glyph blocks in each *t'ol* either do, or at least could, refer to rain. In the third glyph block, two of the three visible compounds are well-known "attribute" glyphs: *kauil* "sustenance" (Stuart 1987:13–16) in *t'ol 4* and *ahauel* "sovereignty" in *t'ol 5.* In *t'ol 1*, the third position has a glyph compound of unknown meaning, *akbal-kin-tun(?)*. Likewise, the meanings of the glyphs in the fourth positions are unclear.

In sum, following the model of parallel syntax presented above, the Paris almanac roughly conforms to a pattern with a subject-attribute sequence. There are apparently no verbs, and therefore no objects in these passages.

In the almanac on page 16, there are two more rain referents in the first glyph block of the two visible *t'ols*. The axe glyph at the top left could mean either "hail" or "lightning." *Baat* is the Yucatec word for "axe," and *baat* is also the Yucatec word for "hail"; but the axe imbedded in the Caban day sign may translate as *hats cah* "strike the land." To strike with an axe is *hats* in Yucatec, and *hats u cah Chac*, as shown above, is glossed as "lightning strikes" in the Motul Dictionary. *Toc*, spelled *to-c(o)*, is the previously discussed strong, brief rain. Beyond this, however, the pattern of subject-attribute is not clear. The common attribute *ahaulil* "sovereignty" is in the top row on page 15, but *yuts* "good," another attribute, is on the bottom row. Likewise, two *chacs* appear in bottom rows, as well as another *baat* "hail" or "lightning," and also *bolon yocte,* a Yucatecan "deity." As in the almanac on pages 17–18, there appear to be no verbs.

SUMMARY

In the Paris almanac section there is one complete 260-day almanac and one or more others beginning on the missing pages to the left. A number of well-known attributes are given, and to some extent there is a syntactic pattern of subject-attribute, but with no verbs. The general subject matter is rain in its many manifestations.

7

Yearbearers

The Paris Codex yearbearer pages are so named because they contain columns of dates that fall on the first day of the Maya 365-day year. *Tuns,* it will be remembered, are periods of 360 days and were part of the intermeshing cycles of *uinals, tuns,* and *katuns* discussed above. But the 365-day year was a separate count, one that closely matched the true solar year. It contained eighteen "months" of twenty days each and an extra five days at the end known as the Uayeb days. (As far as is known, the Maya did not have a leap year.)

Because of the mathematics of concurrently running cycles, only four of twenty day names can land on the first of Pop, the first Maya "month." These four day names are the yearbearers. In the Paris Codex, the days are Lamat, Ben, Edznab, and Akbal, and these can be thought of as a set of yearbearers.

YUCATECAN YEARBEARERS

On the left margin of each of the Paris yearbearer pages, the vertical columns of day signs are mostly missing, but these can be easily reconstructed (Fig. 7.1). Reading from left to right, beginning at the top, the series of yearbearers on these pages can be reconstructed as 5 Lamat, 6 Ben, 7 Edznab, 8 Akbal, 9 Lamat, and so forth, each date being 365 days later than its predecessor. The whole cycle runs fifty-two years to 4 Akbal at the lower right, from where it returns to 5 Lamat at the upper left.

There was another set of yearbearers used in northern Yucatán that was shifted one day (Proskouriakoff and Thompson 1947; Thompson 1950: 127); it was Muluc, Ix, Cauac, and Kan. The Paris and Dresden codices used the former set, the Madrid and Landa's *Relación* give the latter:

| Paris and Dresden: | Lamat | Ben | Edznab | Akbal |
| Madrid and Landa: | Muluc | Ix | Cauac | Kan |

Thompson (1950: 127) worked out a table of corresponding Yucatecan yearbearers and European years. Based on this table, the European years that the Paris New Year pages *could* have covered is presented here. The first yearbearer in the Paris Codex table, 5 Lamat, corresponds to 6 Muluc in Thompson's table, a one-day shift. As a yearbearer, 5 Lamat occurred in 1534; fifty-two years earlier, 5 Lamat was in 1482; therefore, the Paris New Year pages would work for the period 1482–1534. Extrapolating back through time, the following periods are presented below, from Classic times to Spanish contact, for which the Paris pages would work.

A correspondence between Yucatecan and European years can also be worked out for the Madrid Codex pages 34–37 (Fig. 7.2). Although there are many scribal errors in the Madrid bar-and-dot coefficients, the first and last entries, top left and bottom right, are correct. The 10 Cauac at the top of the first column fell in 1564 and every fifty-two years prior to that date. The Dresden Codex (Fig. 7.3) cannot be matched to the European calendar because the yearbearers have no coefficients.

Lamat
years

Ben
years

Edznab
years

Akbal
years

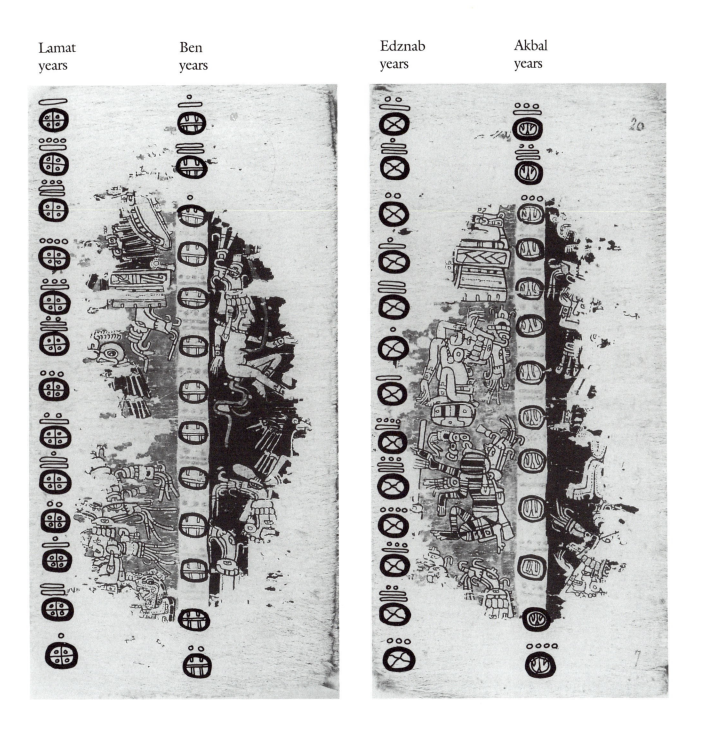

Figure 7.1. Reconstructed yearbearer dates in the Paris Codex. The dates read from top left, 5 Lamat, to bottom right, 4 Akbal. Courtesy of Phot. Bibl. Nat. Paris.

Figure 7.2. "New Year pages" from the Madrid Codex, pages 34–37. Columns of yearbearers form the left margin of each page. Courtesy of Akademische Druck- u. Verlagsanstalt.

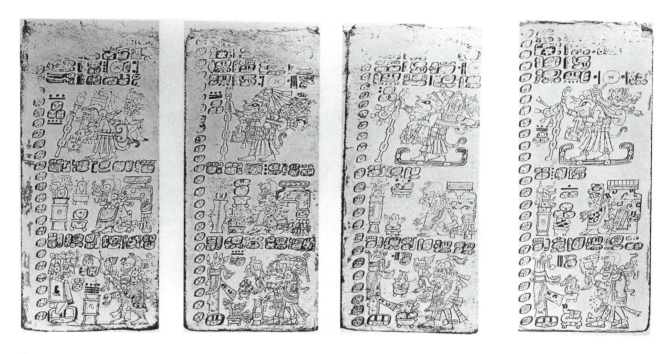

Figure 7.3. New Year pages from the Dresden Codex, pages 25–28. On each page there is a column of day signs at the left margin. The upper half of each column is the last day of the outgoing year repeated thirteen times. The lower half is the first day of the new year—also the yearbearer and the first day of Pop—repeated thirteen times. Courtesy of American Philosophical Society.

Paris	Madrid
1534–1586	1512–1564
1482–1534	1460–1512
1430–1482	1408–1460
1378–1430	1356–1408
1326–1378	1304–1356
1274–1326	1252–1304
1222–1274	1200–1252
1170–1222	1148–1200
1118–1170	1096–1148
1066–1118	1044–1096
1014–1066	996–1044
962–1014	940–996
910–962	888–940

The cycles of fifty-two yearbearers apparently do not have a beginning or end, but run continuously through eternity. The Maya did not, as far as research shows, celebrate the fifty-two-year-period, as did the Aztecs in Central Mexico. Of course, they had the fifty-two-year cycle and were certainly aware of it, but there are no accounts of major ceremonies such as the Aztec New Fire Ceremony that was performed at the end of a fifty-two-year-cycle in Tenochtitlan (present-day Mexico City) in 1507. The analogous Maya time period, where the transition from one "age" to the next marked a change in the cosmic order and was celebrated with great ritual, was the *katun* (discussed above). The different "beginning" dates of the Paris and Madrid yearbearer tables support the claim that no particular fifty-two-year period was celebrated.

From an ethnographic perspective, it seems probable that if a Maya scribe was composing a brand-new sacred book, he would start his yearbearer pages with the current or upcoming year. With no fixed beginning or end to any particular fifty-two-year cycle, one would reasonably start with the present. This could explain why the Paris and the Madrid begin at different points. They were written by different scribes at different times.

NEW YEAR CEREMONIES

As already stated, the Paris, Madrid, and Dresden codices all have pages with columns of yearbearers (Figs. 7.1–7.3). Because yearbearers mark the beginnings of new 365-day years, these pages have loosely been called New Year pages by many Maya scholars. This term is misleading. In Landa's *Relación,* there are, in fact, three kinds of New Year ceremonies (Love 1986:169–204; Tozzer 1941:139) which have often been lumped together in such discussions. They are Uayeb ceremonies held during the final five days of the year that is ending; ceremonies held on the first of Pop to avert calamities for the coming year; and renewal ceremonies held during the month of Pop.

In both the Dresden and Madrid New Year pages, the images represent real ritual paraphernalia and ceremonial activities for humans and gods, as if the books themselves were prescribing the required elements for a well-run ceremony. On the Dresden pages (25–28), it is certain that Uayeb ceremonies are depicted because parts of the scenes match very closely the Uayeb ceremonies described by Landa (Thomas 1882:59–92; Seler 1904:26–35; Förstemann 1906; Thompson 1934, 1972:89–93; Tozzer 1941:134–149; Love 1986:180–201; Taube 1988b:219–245). On the Madrid pages (34–37), important elements of ceremonies are also shown, and, as in the Dresden, many of them match Landa's accounts, but these elements do not fall in Landa's description of Uayeb ceremonies. Rather, they match Landa's descriptions of ceremonies to avert calamities, which are held on the first of Pop, the first day of the first Maya "month."

Some of the matching elements between the Madrid New Year pages and Landa's *Relación* are as follows: a cloth without embroidery; dancing on stilts; dancing (represented by feet in the Madrid) with dogs; a dog with bread on its back; a bound victim thrown from a height onto an altar of stones; a dog with a black spot on its back; singing and playing a drum; and offerings of bread together with headdresses, or miters (Thomas 1882:79–80; Chase 1985:226–232; Love 1986:235–240). In Landa, these all occur in the ceremonies performed on the first of Pop, not during the Uayeb days.

Thus it appears that the Dresden New Year pages deal with Uayeb ceremonies during the last five days of the year that is ending, while the Madrid New Year pages deal with ceremonies on the first of Pop. This explains why the vertical columns of day signs on the Dresden and Madrid pages are different. In the Dresden, there are two day signs on each page, marking the last day of Uayeb and the following day, the first of Pop. In the Madrid, only the yearbearer, the first day of the New Year, is listed.

The Paris pages are altogether different. They are not guides for ceremonies, not pictures of ritual performers with prescribed offerings; instead, the images appear as omens, portents of things to come.

YEARBEARER IMAGES

Taube (1988b:246–253) has presented a detailed iconographic description of the figures from which the following is drawn. For reasons unclear, the background colors alternate, as pointed out by Gates (1910:27): red, black, red, black.

Lamat Years

1. (Beginning at the top) Skeletal death god with jawbone and ribs visible, anus also shown. Seated on rooftop with skyband and maize headdress hanging down.
2. Vulture.
3. God E (Maize God) with elaborate headdress, two maize plants coming out of maize tamale headdress, headband of beads of shell, seated on a *tun* sign.
4. Jaguar devouring a human.

Ben Years

1. Top figure missing, bit of toe showing.
2. Naked God E disemboweled with entrails coming out anus and gash in abdomen.
3. A hook-beaked bird with a curl in its eye, pulling on intestines.
4. God E (Maize God) with a *uah* sign on a kind of pedestal behind him.

Edznab Years

1. Unidentified god sitting on a cloth-fringed rooftop.
2. God E (Maize God) on a *tun* sign with head back, looking up, gesture of "woe" (?).
3. Wrapped figure, possibly a straw-bundle effigy, with a staff or planting stick, maize on

its back, left hand in planting or scattering gesture.
4. Two Maize Gods facing each other.

Akbal Years

1. Open-mouthed jaguar in pouncing position.
2. God E (Maize God) with a necklace, pendant, perhaps being attacked.
3. Seated unidentified animal, paws similar to those of a jaguar, but also similar to seated dogs in Madrid New Year pages.
4. God E (Maize God) with "woe" (?) hand position, with jaguar paw on forehead, probably being attacked by a jaguar.

READING THE YEARBEARERS

Each set of yearbearer dates is accompanied by figures allowing the Maya priest, the Ah Kin, to assign omens and auguries to the prescribed years. This is reminiscent of Landa's description of forecasts for the Cauac years: "This year, in addition to the predicted mortality, they regard as unfortunate, since they said that many hot suns would destroy the fields of maize, and that the many ants and birds would devour the seeds, which they sowed. And as this would not happen everywhere, there would be food in some places, which they could get with a great deal of labor" (Tozzer 1941:148).

Most of the images on the Paris yearbearer pages are Maize Gods. Their condition, whether strong and healthy or vulnerable and debilitated, reflects the precarious circumstances of Maya existence in which the vicissitudes of rain, sun, wild animals, and spirit protectors hold dominion over maize, the soul of Maya life.

Intertwining and meshing are the keys to understanding Maya prognostication (Love 1992). Barbara Tedlock's (1982, 1992) work in Momostenango illuminates the complexities of calendar specialists at work. Whole years are colored by the personalities of the yearbearers, Mams in Highland Guatemala, but the Mams themselves are ranked—Quej being the first and most important. When a day-keeper in Momostenango divines the meaning of a day in the 260-day sacred round, the reading is influenced by the yearbearer for that year. If the yearbearer is a negative force, an inauspicious reading becomes even more severely ill-omened, and if a diviner, counting through the sacred round, comes to rest on a yearbearer's name day, all significance is intensified. Tedlock has shown that the number joined to the day name in the 260-day count has its effect, too; the lower numbers are rather weak, the higher numbers strong.

When searching for auspicious days in the almanacs (in the God C pages, for instance), the Ah Kin can add another layer of meaning to his findings and deepen his understanding of the spirit forces at work by including a reference to the yearbearer pages. Omens for the day Lamat, for example, are intensified if that particular Lamat falls in a year that has one of the Lamats for a yearbearer. It is magnified further if the Lamat year has an auspicious number attached. But a Lamat falling in an Akbal year would have only average meaning, and its augury could be offset by other forces. For the Maya priest using the Paris Codex, the yearbearer pages are an integral part of the whole.

SUMMARY

The Paris Codex yearbearer pages present a fifty-two-year tableau of dates and corresponding omens. The day signs with their bars and dots are in fact spirit entities, with the yearbearers themselves laden with meaning. Their interpretation by the Maya priest colors his understanding and interpretation of other parts of the codex. The central issue seems to be the all-consuming concern over the health of the maize crop.

8

Day-Sign Tables

Dominating the left two-thirds of page 21 of the Paris Codex are columns of day signs, individual days from the Maya 260-day sacred calendar. It is not altogether clear whether the left two-thirds of page 21 (Fig. 8.1) form a separate section from the "spirit world" page (see Chapter 9) to its right. The green cords, identical to the cords on the following page, argue for the sections being joined. Likewise, the rows of glyphs at the top of the two pages may run together. Arguing for separation of the sections is the vertical rope just to the right of the daysigns, which falls in line with the black vertical lines descending from the bird head just below, forming a division that runs to the bottom of the page. To the right of this vertical division, the red background and the figures facing to the right suggest that they are part of the scene on page 22. At the bottom of the page, the figures left of the vertical line are part of the day-sign section above it and appear not to be related to the spirit-world scenes to the right. Therefore, this chapter deals with the left two-thirds of page 21 as if it is a section to itself.

HIEROGLYPHS

Beginning on this page and continuing for the next three pages, the hieroglyphs all appear in "reverse" order. They are facing to the right and are to be read from right to left, but it is not known whether they should be read down in single columns, in double columns, or horizontally across. A few of the phonetic signs are known, but complete readings remain a problem. Most glyphs are familiar to students of Maya writing, but comprehensible interpretations elude us, such as the bar-and-dot number six (*uac*) over

a *yax* sign attached to a *uinic* sign with an affix, probably a *na,* over it. *Uac yax na uinic* makes no sense.

DAY-SIGN CALCULATIONS

Within the green borders lie some fourteen sets of day signs, each set being a column of five (Fig. 8.2). Across the center of the field are some black numbers. The simplest solution to understanding these numbers is a suggestion by Charles Bowditch, relegated to a footnote in William Gates's commentary: "Mr. Bowditch suggests to me that the numbers 1 2 3 3 5 6 6 are to be read with each of the daysigns in their respective columns, and, being placed in the middle, may apply both to the upper and lower sets" (Gates 1910:29). In the top right-hand column of day names (Fig. 8.2), the series runs, from bottom to top, 1 Ben, 1 Chicchan, 1 Caban, 1 Muluc, 1 Imix, then back to 1 Ben, completing a 260-day round. The value of the number does not affect the internal consistency of each column. Any number from one to thirteen could be used with any of the given columns of five day signs as long as the same number was read with each of the signs. The columns would still total the same number of days.

As mentioned, the right-hand column is a 260-day round. The other columns, to the left, can be read in two ways, both of which are meaningful and functional. Reading from the bottom up, there is a 104-day interval or a 364-day interval between each sign. For example, in the second column from the right (Fig. 8.2), the series begins 2 Manik. Counting through the *tsolkin,* the calendar priest arrives at the next sign up in the column, 2 Chuen, 104 days later. But if he added

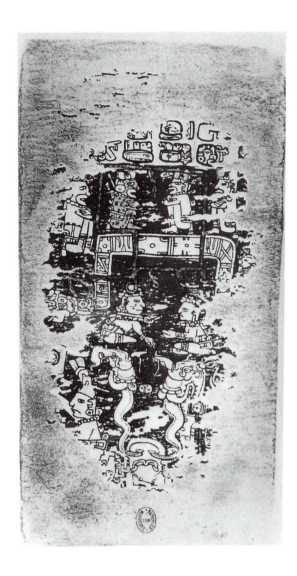

Figure 8.1. The division between the day-sign section, *left,* and the spirit-world section. Courtesy of Phot. Bibl. Nat. Paris.

another complete *tsolkin* to his count before stopping, he would still arrive at 2 Chuen. In other words, the signs can be thought of as 104 days apart or 364 (104 + 260) days apart. In this way, the whole column can serve a double function. When the intervals are read as 104 days, a single column makes a total round of 520 days, a double *tsolkin*. When the signs are read as 364 days apart, the total for the column is 1,820 days, or seven *tsolkins,* a cycle found heading a quadruple almanac in the Dresden Codex (Fig. 8.3) and a cycle laid out in the constellation pages (see Chapter 10).

In the lower divisions (Fig. 8.2), the col-

umns also read from the bottom up. Again the right column has 260 days with five 52-day intervals, while the others are 520- (or 1,820-) day cycles. Two of the columns, however (the third and fourth from the right), do not have five intervals of 104 days but instead have two intervals of 156 days and two of 52 days. This may or may not have been intentional. The total number of days is still 520.

In the scheme just presented, each column works as an independent round. Perhaps a pattern of numbers joins the columns so that the specialist could go from one to another, but it is

Figure 8.2. The sets of day signs on page 21 of the Paris Codex. Courtesy of Phot. Bibl. Nat. Paris.

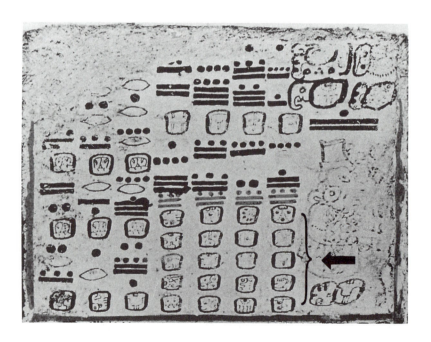

Figure 8.3. Day-sign columns from the Dresden Codex, page 32a; the number thirteen at the top of each column is to be read with each of the numbers in the column. Reading down, the signs are 364 days apart; altogether, an 1,820-day cycle is recorded. It stands at the head of a Chac almanac dealing with weather. Courtesy of American Philosophical Society.

Figure 8.4. Almanac from the Dresden Codex, pages 6c–7c, with the same day-sign divisions as the bottom right column on the Paris day-sign page. Courtesy of American Philosophical Society.

not evident. Knorozov (1982:207–208) attempts to read the signs horizontally from right to left, producing a single table of 25 × 364, but his conclusions are invalidated by his extensive reconstructions of supposed scribal errors and, most damning, his misreading of Akbal for Chuen at the bottom of the far left column in the top division.

READING THE DAY-SIGN COLUMNS

The general format of having numbers at the head of columns of day signs is found throughout the Maya codices at the beginnings of almanacs (see Chapter 6). The numbers at the tops of almanac columns are read with each of the day signs below them. The difference here is that the columns read from bottom to top instead of top to bottom. In the Dresden Codex on page 32a (Fig. 8.3), there are four columns of day signs reminiscent of the day-sign table in the Paris Codex. The Dresden example has red thirteens at the top of each column. The thirteens are to be read with each of the signs below them (Thompson 1972:94–95).

The day-sign columns in the Paris Codex may be thought of as disembodied almanacs, almanacs for which the principal divisions are

given, but without their *t'ols*. They could stand for distinct single or double *tsolkins*—a shorthand reference to complete almanacs fully drawn out elsewhere in the codex or in other codices. For example, there is a 260-day almanac in the Dresden Codex on pages 6c–7c (Fig. 8.4) which has the same day signs as the bottom right column in the Paris. Likewise, the far left column in the upper division in the Paris begins, at the bottom of the column, with 6 Chuen. The next sign up is 6 Men, a 104-day interval, indicating a 520-day cycle. This same cycle is found in both the Madrid (10a–13a) and the Dresden (38b–41b) in 520-day almanacs (Fig. 8.5).

As previously mentioned, two columns have 52- and 156-day intervals within the same column. These could not function at the head of typical almanacs which, of course, require consistently repeating intervals, so incorporting these into the system is a problem.

THE IMAGES BELOW THE DAY SIGNS

The illustrations in the lower division of this page are integrated into the whole. An intertwined cord, which surrounds the day-sign columns above, descends through a skyband into the scene below and loops around a *kin* sign.

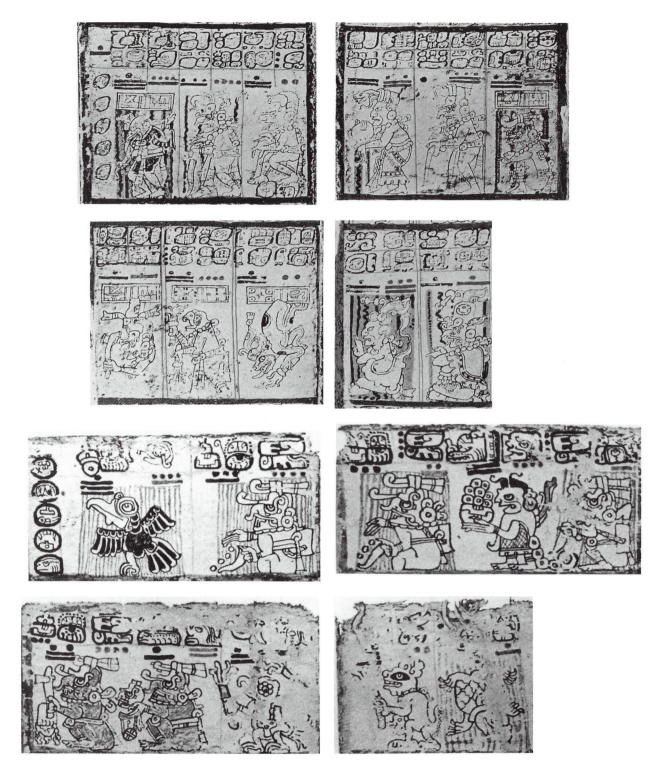

Figure 8.5. Chac almanacs from, *above,* the Dresden Codex, pages 38b–41b, and, *below,* the Madrid Codex, pages 10a–13a. Each almanac is 520 days and is headed by the same day signs as one of the columns on the Paris day-sign page. They deal with weather, including torrential downpours. Dresden Codex courtesy of American Philosophical Society. Madrid Codex courtesy of Akademische Druck- u. Verlagsanstalt.

Figure 8.6. Ancestor cartouche from the east side of the Palace at Palenque (Maudslay 1889–1902: vol. 4, Plate 6).

Four serpent heads protrude from the loop, forming in effect a cartouche, not unlike the "ancestor cartouches" (Fig. 8.6) on the east side of the Palace at Palenque (Maudslay 1889–1902: vol. 4, Plate 6; Tozzer 1957: Figs. 267, 268). Behind the serpent head cartouche, rain falls with the word *toc* (*to-co*) spelled in it, indicating a *toc chac* type of rain, a fierce, brief downpour (see Chapter 6). Poised below is a devouring or attacking serpent.

To the left of the downpour is a separate scene, without rain, in which a death god, identified by his skulllike forehead and death-eyes bracelet, smokes an upturned cigar and holds a flaming torch (Taube, personal communication, 1986). To the right, facing toward the attacking serpent, is a figure called a black God D by Gates (1910: 29) and a black god with the face of an old man, possibly God N, by Förstemann (1906: 37). Taube (1988b) points out the similarities with the black-faced god in the Dresden page with a torrential downpour.

SUMMARY

The day-sign columns are surrounded by green sky cords which intertwine, descend, and encircle a *kin* sign, meaning "day" or "sun." That day or sun is in a torrential downpour. By extension, all the days in the columns above are in downpours. If the columns serve as heads of almanacs, they are almanacs dealing with rain. One of the columns is found at the beginnings of 520-day almanacs in the Dresden and Madrid codices (Fig. 8.5). These almanacs show many *t'ols* with torrential rainstorms just like the one falling around the *kin* sign in the Paris. Thus, this page of the Paris Codex, like the almanac and God C pages, deals with weather.

9

The Spirit World

As mentioned in Chapter 8, the right side of page 21 and all of page 22 of the Paris Codex probably form a single scene (see Fig. 8.1). This is suggested by the continuous red background and the body positions of the two visible figures on page 21, who face into the scene on page 22. The scene is a composite visualization of at least part of the Maya spirit world.

PAUAHTUNS

The four figures at the top of the spirit-world scene are Pauahtuns (Fig. 9.1), beings associated with rains, winds, and the four world directions. Their identification in the Paris Codex is based on their headdresses (Coe 1973:14–15), which contain the *uah* element (Taube 1989b). They are seated with their arms folded, as pointed out by Förstemann (1903:38), indicating a resting posture or a nonaction attitude.

The Pauahtuns are among the most durable spirit beings in all of Maya religion. They are found in pre-Hispanic Maya art, Colonial Period sources, and twentieth-century rituals. In historical sources from Yucatán, the term is divided into two words, *Pauah* and *tun*. It is found thus divided in the Landa manuscript (1566:fol. 28v) and in the Chilam Balam of Chumayel (Gordon 1913:51, 56).

In the New Year ceremonies described by Landa (Tozzer 1941:137–138), four yearbearers held dominion over succeeding years; in turn, each yearbearer was associated with various omens (see Chapter 7). The principal omen, or destiny, of a year was the Bacab of that year, a spirit ruler associated with a specific color and world direction. Accompanying the Bacabs were, among other beings, Chacs and Pauahtuns. Like the Bacabs and the Chacs, there were four Pauahtuns, each associated with colors and directions.

Pauahtuns appear in the Chilam Balam of Chumayel (Fig. 9.2) as four wind spirits (Gordon 1913:51), translated by Roys as "angels of the winds" (Roys 1933:110). In nineteenth-century Yucatán, a Spanish priest observed a native agricultural ceremony that he called a "milpa mass," a ritual performed for the maize fields. In the Maya prayers, the leader of the ceremony addressed four spirits known as *pahahtun* [sic]. They were red, white, black, and yellow, and were identified as the guardians of the rains (Baeza 1845:170).

In the twentieth century, two ethnographic studies in small Maya villages recorded prayers to these same spirits. They were petitioned in agricultural ceremonies in Chan Kom (Redfield and Villa 1934:354–355), transcribed *pahuatun;* and in Quintana Roo they were found in prayers of the Cruzob Maya and were called *papatuns* (Villa 1945:159). Barrera Vásquez, author of numerous scholarly works on Maya culture and the principal author of the Cordemex Maya-Spanish Dictionary, reports that *babah tuns* are sometimes addressed by modern shamans (Barrera Vásquez 1976:38), a point amply confirmed by John Sosa's fieldwork in Yalcobá (Sosa 1985:454, 460–463). Such a continuous presence in the Maya ritual mentality, from the pre-Hispanic period to the present, underscores the Pauahtuns' essential role in Maya religion.

Like their counterparts in the ethnohistorical record, each of the four Pauahtuns on page 22 is distinct. Although their colors have faded, one is clearly green, the Yax (green) Pauahtun. The

Figure 9.1. Pauahtuns in the Paris Codex. Courtesy of Phot. Bibl. Nat. Paris.

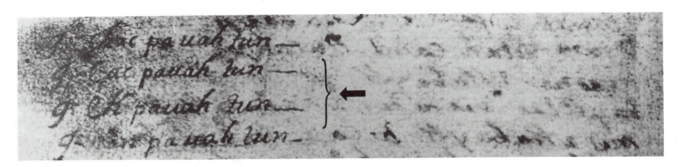

Figure 9.2. Pauahtuns in the Chilam Balam of Chumayel. Each is a different color: *chac*, red; *sac*, white; *ek*, black; and *kan*, yellow (Gordon 1913:51).

others each wear distinctive apparel, be it head-dress, ear ornament, or body clothing. Their position in the sky, above the skyband, is appropriate considering their association with the winds and rains (Roys 1933:170–171; Thompson 1934).

OTHER SPIRITS

To the left are two standing or striding figures (Fig. 8.1). Both are spotted green, the lower one having a double curved stripe. Though it is not clear what they are doing, the lower one is reaching up, possibly to the end of one of the sky-ropes.

In the center of page 22, framed by the sky-band above and the devouring serpents below, are two death gods identified by "death-eye" collars, bone headdresses, and a "percent sign" on the cheek of one. Their animated gestures show

that they are interacting or communicating with each other. Although they carry the attributes of death gods, they are quite alive, reminiscent of gods who are conferring in some scenes in the Dresden Codex (Fig. 9.3).

In the lower left portion of page 22 is an unidentified youthful god, probably sitting, with his right arm extended upward. Just below him is a partial rendering of a skeletal profile. Both figures face to the left. Just to the right of the skyband is a light green arm and hand reaching up and grabbing part of the green skyrope.

OTHER IMAGES

Two menacing serpents in the lower center of the page have emerged from the eyes of a death head or skull that has unusual lips. Like the serpent below the *kin* cartouche on the day-sign page,

 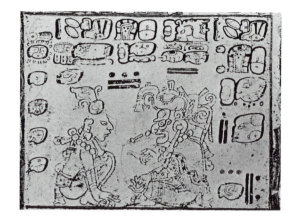

Figure 9.3. Gods conferring in the Dresden Codex, pages 8b–9b. Their positions are similar to those of the death gods in the Paris spirit-world section. Courtesy of American Philosophical Society.

and like the open-jawed animals in the constellation pages that follow, these serpents are threatening or attacking.

Between the serpents, suspended in space, is an inverted Ahau sign of unknown meaning. Also visible are two *kin* signs in dark and light fields (discussed in Chapter 10). The sun sign to the lower right is attached to the end of a green skyrope, and more skyrope is visible to its right and above it, twisting and curling.

NUMBER COLUMN

At the extreme lower right of the page, a column of numbers is barely visible (Fig. 9.4). Number columns like these have a long history in Maya art, dating at least from the Classic Period. On certain monuments there is an association between a glyph that has the appearance of a gopher head with signs for trees and columns of numbers. In examples at Copan and Tikal, a gopher-head glyph, a tree, and a number column are conflated into single signs (Figure 9.4).

There are similar number columns in the Madrid Codex. In one Madrid example (page 73b), the number column is suspended from the upper lip of a long-nosed Chac figure with an inkbrush and inkpot in hand (Figure 9.4). Presumably, the hanging number scroll is an identifying marker for scribes, or perhaps it identifies the art of writing (Coe 1977:331). But in other cases, the function of the numbers is less easily interpreted. On Madrid pages 57a and 69a, they appear on what seem to be trees. The Madrid 57 example has a flower growing from its side and a hummingbird reaching its beak up to it. The Madrid 69 example has a flower at its top along with a *che* or *te* "tree" sign at the base. The bumps on the outline of the two "trees" are standard symbols for wooden objects.

In another Madrid example (Figure 9.4), the number column takes the shape of the seat on which a god holds a maize offering. In this case, the moon sign for "twenty" can be seen, as well as an unidentified spiral sign, which must also be a number. The moon sign is twenty; the spiral may be a shell representing zero.

In the Paris number column, there is also a figure, presumably representing a number, that is neither the moon sign nor the shell, and it remains unidentified. Gates (1910:30) saw a 13 Ahau here—the double vertical lines at the top of the sign are similar to the Ahau day signs on the constellation pages.

To date, no satisfactory interpretation of the numbers either here or in the Madrid has been offered. Without finding the significance of these numbers, their reading must remain speculation. In the Paris example one finds, reading from the top, a thirteen, a possible Ahau sign, a possible two, and a six. It is tempting to think that the numbers are generic in nature—representing the idea of counting or writing—and not real dates or true counts. Such a suggestion, however, ex-

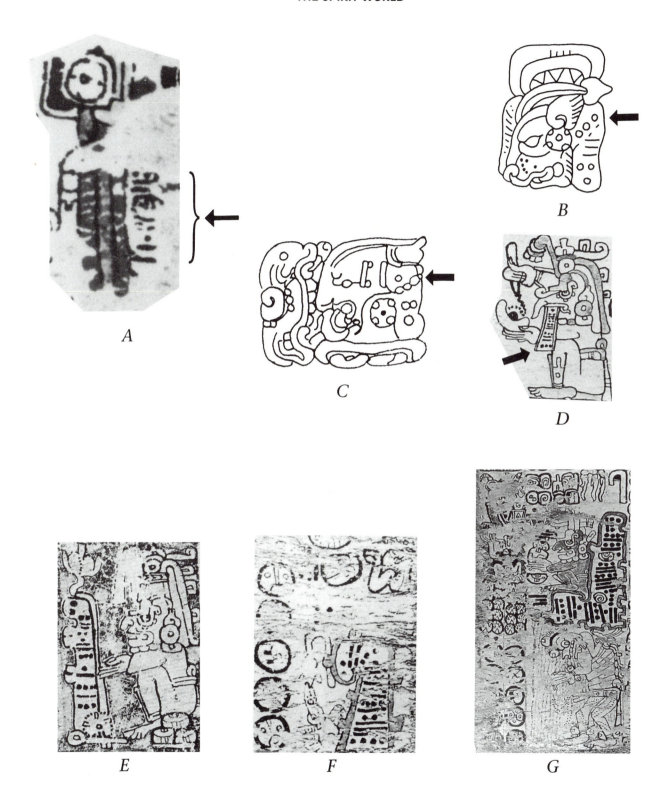

Figure 9.4. Number columns. *A,* Paris Codex, page 22; *B,* Copan Stela 2, after drawing by Barbara Fash; *C,* Lintel 3, Tikal Structure 5c-4 (Temple IV) after drawing by William Coe, Tikal Report 33, Fig. 74 (Jones and Satterthwaite 1982); *D,* Madrid Codex, page 73; *E,* Madrid Codex, page 57a; *F,* Madrid Codex, page 69a; *G,* Madrid Codex, page 8. Paris Codex courtesy of Phot. Bibl. Nat. Paris; Madrid Codex courtesy of Akademische Druck- u. Verlagsanstalt.

Figure 9.5. The Palenque sarcophagus lid. Photograph by Merle Greene Robertson.

Figure 9.6. Tulum mural, Structure 5, showing twisted cord (Miller 1982: Plate 37). Courtesy of Dumbarton Oaks.

cuses the researcher from further investigation. It is more productive to adopt the working hypothesis that the Maya scribe was specifying true counts and, with that supposition, begin to fathom his meaning.

THE INTEGRATED COSMOS

Up to this point many diverse features in this complex scene have been described separately and in some detail. But the scene should be viewed in its entirety as a unified whole. The Maya artist has created an integrating effect by literally tying the scene together with skyropes. The skyband, probably the double-headed variety (Carlson 1988; Carlson and Landis 1985), divides the cosmos, with the Pauahtuns above, in space, and the death gods below in the gaping jaws of serpent creatures that are writhing forth from the hollow eyes

of death itself. One is reminded, in the sense of spatial organization, of the Palenque sarcophagus carving of Lord Pacal perched within the skeletal jaws of the earth or death monster, while birds, trees, and symbols of life fill the sky above (Fig. 9.5).

Here in the Paris, the opposing realms of life and death are tied together by celestial cords which transit through the skyband, passing by, encircling, touching, and being held by the deities of sky and earth. Similar cords in the Tulum murals (Fig. 9.6) have been interpreted by Arthur Miller as "physical links between the upper registers and lower ones, bands that represent the Upperworld and Underworld . . . " (Miller 1982:95). There is a scene in Landa's account of sixteenth-century Yucatán in which performers impersonating Chacs stretch a long rope around a sacred space for a "baptism" ceremony (Tozzer

1941:102–106). In another scene groups of men pass a common rope through their penises, binding themselves together in blood sacrifice (ibid.: 114). In more recent times, Villa Rojas reported that the Maya of Quintana Roo in the 1930s believed that in ancient times a "living rope" in the air linked all the Maya cities of Yucatán and that this rope could be traveled on (Sullivan 1989: 85). As Cecelia Klein has said (1982:2), the sacred cords' "common function lies in their ability to connect disparate points and thus provide a means of passage and communication. . . ." Thus the Paris Codex skyropes unify and integrate an otherwise disjointed cosmos.

SUMMARY

The Maya spirit world is a realm of invisible powers affecting all aspects of life. The surviving images in the Paris Codex show some twelve deity-like figures, either complete or fragmentary, along with a serpent skyband, a death image, sun signs, and part of an enigmatic number series. The whole picture is intertwined with green cords. The scene, taken as a whole, is a visual manifestation of Maya phantom forces.

10

Signs of the Night

Pages 23 and 24 of the Paris Codex are often called the zodiac pages, but it would be better to call them the constellation pages. The zodiac is a band about eighteen degrees wide across the sky. To the ground-based observer, the sun, the moon, and the visible planets travel within this path, rising in the east, passing overhead, and setting in the west. Certain constellations, spaced around the band, mark divisions or points along the band. These constellations are used to designate the stations, or houses, of the zodiac. The Maya probably did not recognize the zodiacal band as an astronomical construct. Stars and groupings of stars were extremely potent forces, and yearly movements of constellations held great meaning, but these stars did not have to lie within the zodiacal band. Orion, in our nomenclature, was the great turtle constellation to the ancient Maya (Lounsbury 1982:166–167) and appears in the Paris constellation pages, but Orion lies outside the zodiac proper, several degrees south of the true zodiacal band.

Following Barbara Tedlock's work in Momostenango (Tedlock 1992:179–185), the constellations found in the Paris Codex are better understood as "signs of the night" (ibid.:182), *retal ak'ab,* in the Quiché language. The signs of the night portend ritual and agricultural phases of the year. The Paris Codex constellation pages present a succession of thirteen such stars or constellations, integrated with a table of 1,820 days (Fig. 10.1).

THE GLYPHS

The glyphs at the top of the two pages face to the right, as they do on the preceding two pages, in-dicating that their reading order is from right to left. The number of columns of glyphs, thirteen, suggests that they should be read as single columns. If each column refers to one of the thirteen signs of the night, then each column would be read separately from the other columns and each would be an independent text. Several of the glyphs have known phonetic readings or are otherwise identifiable, but the texts as a whole cannot be understood at this time. In fact, even the reading order is unclear. In the second and third columns, the pairing of Itzamna's name glyph and the Ahau glyph (inverted) with two *li* signs (read Itzamna Ahaulil?) is a common name compound in the Maya codices. The side-by-side position of this compound, spanning two columns, suggests that the text may be read in double columns or even horizontal rows. This whole section of glyphs must await further advances in decipherment before its meaning becomes clear.

THE SKYBANDS

The upper skyband on the constellation pages is a rather typical bicephalic sky monster (Carlson and Landis 1985:138). As noted by Spinden (1916:74–75), at the far left on page 23 the band turns down sharply, probably leading to one of the dragon's heads. At the far right, no such bend is visible, but there is enough room in the erased part of the page to accommodate another turn downward to another dragon head. This is comparable to the skyband in the previous spirit world pages. The skyband forms a wide celestial canopy over the panel beneath it. Below the day-sign table that lies across the center of the pages

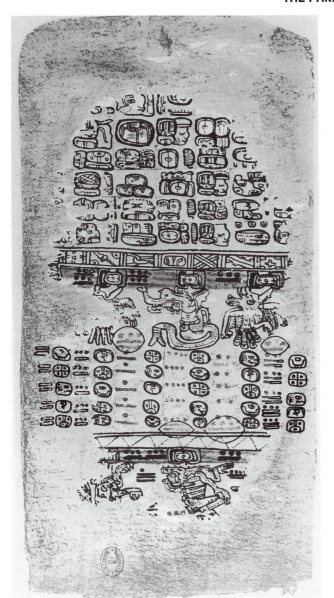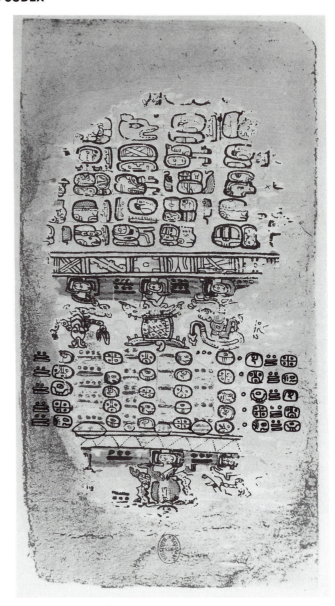

Figure 10.1. Paris Codex constellation pages with reconstructed day signs in the 1,820-day table. The green correction numbers are circled. Original courtesy of Phot. Bibl. Nat. Paris.

is another band with a diamond pattern of dotted lines, probably a symbol for snake, or *can. Can,* in Yucatec Mayan, means snake and *caan* (sometimes *ca'an*) means sky. *Kin* signs and animal figures hang from this lower band in the same way they hang from the skyband above.

BLACK EIGHTS

The modern student will see that there are black bar-and-dot eights just below each of the bands.

Several attempts at understanding the Maya use of these have been less than satisfying. The numbers are stacked, eight over eight, below the upper skyband, but appear singly or side by side below the lower band. A sixteen, a fourteen, and some other numbers also appear below the lower band. Where they are stacked, the Maya number 0.8.8 (168) could be inferred. The significance of the number 168 is that it is 6 × 28, and 28 days is the interval between the day signs in the table of day signs in the center of the page. Kelley

(1976:49–50) suggests that the animal figures, representing constellations in a zodiac, are separated by 168 days or twice that number, 336 days, and that alternate pictures are one-third to one-half of the sky apart. Lounsbury (in Justeson 1989:117) has also suggested that the animal figures are separated by 168 days. In fact, if the animal figures in the top row are separated by 28 days, a model proposed here, then each animal (except the erased one at the far right) is separated by 168 days from the animal figure below it, in the bottom row. But none of these explanations takes into account the lower register, where other numbers appear and where black eights are not stacked. Further speculation without showing a clear solution would be of little service at this point.

SUN SIGNS

The sun signs, *kin* in Yucatec Mayan, have dark and light framed areas on either side of them and open-mouthed animals below. These repeat seven times across the upper skyband that spans the two pages. The one on the far right is erased but is assumed to have been present based on a fragmentary outline of a figure below it. Aligned below the diamond band, or lower skyband, five more *kin* signs appear, but the original total cannot be determined. There is room for two more figures on page 23 on the left and right sides, and room for one more on page 24 on the right side. At the bottom far right there is only the barest of lines where a figure might have been. So the total number of *kin* signs with animals is not definitely known, but the easiest "fit" would be three on each page. The total, then, was probably thirteen, seven above and six below, and the following discussion proceeds on that assumption.

THE ECLIPSE GLYPH

The *kin* sign with dark and light fields (Fig. 10.2) is often interpreted as a sign for solar eclipses. In the same way, when the moon glyph replaces the sun glyph in the same dark and light fields, it is interpreted as a lunar eclipse (Fig. 10.2). The eclipse interpretation is widely held by students of Maya writing and iconography, but, following David Kelley (1976:43, 52), one might discard

this interpretation for several reasons.

In all four surviving Maya codices, there is one generally accepted eclipse table, pages 51–58 in the Dresden Codex. There is virtually unanimous agreement among researchers that these pages record eclipse "windows," dates when eclipses could occur. Most say that the pages deal with solar eclipses (Makemson 1943:191; Lounsbury 1978:798; Bricker and Bricker 1983), but some say they could have been solar or lunar, with lunar being more likely (Thompson 1972:71–77; Aveni 1980). On an ethnographic level, a lunar interpretation seems much more likely because, as Aveni (1980) points out, a lunar table could be compiled by native priests in about one generation of eclipse watching, while it would take hundreds of years of recording solar eclipses to devise a prediction table. Justeson (1989:84) has shown how two or three decades of lunar eclipse observations could produce a complete system of successful lunar eclipse predictions and that such a system would be structured like the one in the Dresden Codex. A lunar table would have about a 50 percent success rate in predicting visible eclipses of the moon, whereas a solar eclipse table would predict *visible* solar eclipses only about 6 percent of the time. Even if a table of solar eclipses could be invented, it would not seem to be particularly useful because it would relate to events that almost never occurred within view of the Mayas.

Whether the eclipse table deals with lunar or solar eclipses makes little difference to the argument here, which is that the so-called eclipse glyph is not necessarily an eclipse glyph. On Maya monuments, there is only one occurrence of this glyph with a known solar eclipse date, at the site of Santa Elena Poco Uinic, Chiapas, and even there the glyph is not clearly the glyph in question (Lounsbury 1978:815–816). There is universal agreement that a series of eclipses is presented on the Dresden Codex pages, but as Kelley points out (1976:43), with all the glyph passages accompanying these tables, it should not be hard to find the glyph for "eclipse," while in fact no glyph is consistently repeated in the texts or in the pictures.

The *kin* sign with flanking dark and light areas appears in the pictures on pages 52b, 54b,

Figure 10.2. Sun sign, *top,* from the Paris Codex. Sun and moon signs, *bottom,* are paired with no eclipse association in the Dresden Codex, page 66a. Courtesy of American Philosophical Society.

56b, and 57b of the Dresden eclipse tables (Fig. 10.3). These tables calculate either lunar or solar eclipses—they were not designed to do both (although in rare cases a lunar and solar eclipse can occur fourteen or fifteen days apart). Above three of the nine illustrations which mark eclipse points in the table, solar and lunar signs are paired, even though eclipses of the sun and the moon could not have occurred on the same date.

Pairings of sun and moon signs with dark and light fields are found throughout the codices in contexts not associated with eclipses, as they are in an almanac in the Dresden Codex dealing with Chacs (Fig. 10.2). In fact, their occurrence in almanacs is a very strong argument against eclipse interpretations. Almanacs are repeating 260-day cycles. They were used continuously, year after year, to divine the fates and forces of particular days. If an eclipse occurred during one of these 260 days, it would not occur again 260 days later. If the Maya scribe recorded an eclipse in one of these passages, it would constrain that passage to be used only once. It would not be valid the next time around. In the Dresden Codex table, where an eclipse prediction function is generally accepted, the eclipse glyph does not occur consistently, but in the Paris constellation pages (Fig. 10.1), where the so-called eclipse glyph appears repeatedly at regular intervals, there are no calculations or patterns of dates that resemble anything like eclipse periods. As discussed below, the day signs make up five rows of 364 days, giving a total of 1,820. No period of 364 days or even 1,820 days could accommodate thirteen eclipses, solar or lunar. In sum, the "eclipse glyph" may be used in association with eclipse dates, but it may also be found in contexts not referring to eclipses. It is not strictly a glyph for eclipses.

A further note on supposed eclipse signs. When sun or moon signs with dark and light fields occur poised above open-jawed animals or monsters, as they do in the Paris Codex constellation pages, the "eclipse" interpretation is thought to be reinforced, because the Yucatec Mayan phrase for solar eclipse is *u chi'bil kin* "the eating of the sun" (Closs 1989). The problem with this argument is that "devouring" serpents, like the supposed eclipse images, appear in many contexts that are not associated with eclipses—for example, the "serpent number" pages (61–62) in the Dresden Codex (Fig. 10.4) and the spirit-world pages in the Paris Codex. It makes more sense to interpret these creatures as threatening or otherwise powerfully influencing the sun. The open-jawed creatures are powerful influences, not devourers.

A better interpretation of the sun or moon signs inside dark and light fields is that they represent the sun or the moon positioned in the sky. The sun sign poised between dark and light fields may represent the sun between night sky and day sky, poised on the horizon between night and day. It is perhaps darkened, but not necessarily eclipsed. When the sun sign and moon sign are paired, as so often occurs in hieroglyphic passages, it can simply be interpreted as a poetic couplet, "the sun and the moon" (Fig. 10.2). When the sun or moon sign with light and dark fields is threatened by an open-jawed beast, the interpretation is that the day or night is threatened; it is a time of danger.

ZODIAC INTERPRETATIONS

Each of the sun signs spaced along the two horizontal bands in the Paris Codex has an animal figure with gaping jaws directly below it. Having shown that these do not represent eclipses, one turns to the interpretation that the animals in question represent an ancient Maya zodiac.

As noted earlier, the zodiac is a belt across the heavens with the sun's path as its center line. The belt is wide enough to include the paths of the moon and the planets. In different cultures around the world, this path is divided into sections named for the principal constellations within them. At any given time, the sun, moon, or any planet is in some house or section of the zodiacal belt. A ground-based observer, like a Maya calendar specialist, can easily see in which part of the celestial band the moon and the planets lie. The Chinese developed a zodiac of some twenty-seven or twenty-eight stations, or "mansions," that the moon passed through, each named for a constellation within it.

Did the Maya recognize a zodiac? The Paris Codex has played a pivotal role in this question for most of the twentieth century because re-

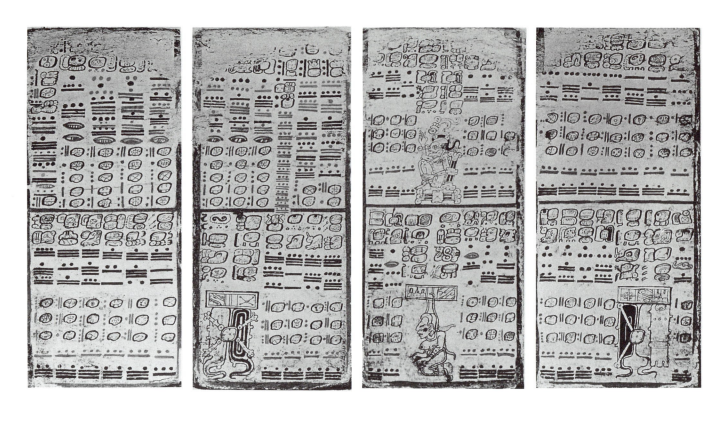

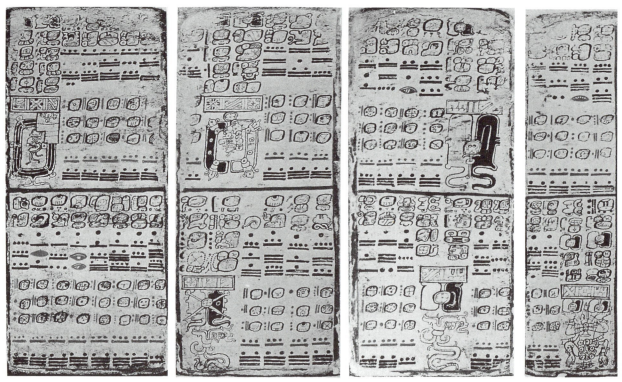

Figure 10.3. Eclipse tables from the Dresden Codex, pages 51–58. Courtesy of American Philosophical Society.

Figure 10.4. Open-jawed snakes without eclipse associations, Dresden Codex, pages 61–62. Courtesy of American Philosophical Society.

searchers have long thought the animals on these pages must surely represent constellations. The intellectual narrative begins with Eduard Seler.

In Seler's "The Animal Pictures of the Mexican and Maya Manuscripts," a section of his classic work (1902–1923, vol. 4), two key observations are made. First, the animal pictures in the Paris Codex are "clearly supposed to be constellations" (ibid., 4:640; Bowditch 1939: vol. 4, p.61); and, second, there is a similar series of animals on the Monjas building at Chichén Itzá (Fig. 10.5) that also represents constellations. In the Chichén Itzá series, there are star signs which Seler interpreted as Venus signs. They are conjoined with animal pictures, which led Seler to believe that the Maya were marking the position of Venus in the zodiac. Kelley (1976:38–42) has convincingly argued that the "Venus" symbol is really the sign for "star" in a generic sense, including stars and planets, not a specific sign for Venus. The star glyph can be used for Venus, but its use is not exclusively reserved for that planet.

Why are the animal representations, in Seler's words, "clearly supposed to be constella-tions"? First, because they are attached to sky-bands and, second, because it is known that the Maya did recognize some constellations as animals. A century ago, Daniel Brinton (1895:35) noted that, among other astronomical terms, the sixteenth-century Motul Dictionary gave an entry for *Mehen Ek* "son star" (Martínez Hernández 1929:624), which was apparently Castor and Pollux, as *los astillejos*, two stars in today's Gemini (Brinton says Orion, Barrera Vásquez [1980:516] says Pleiades). There was another listing for three unidentified stars, in the sixteenth-century sign of Gemini, called *Ac* or *Ac Ek* "turtle star" (Martínez Hernández 1929:66). Landa says the Maya of sixteenth-century Yucatán used the Pleiades and Gemini as nighttime guides to the rising of Venus (Tozzer 1941:132–133). A number of dictionaries (Barrera Vásquez 1980:849) list *tsab,* the rattles of the rattlesnake, as the name for the Pleiades, and *zinaan ek* is in the Motul Dictionary (Martínez Hernández 1929:237) and other dictionaries as "Scorpion, sign of the sky." It is not known whether the Maya "scorpion" was the same group of stars as the European constellation

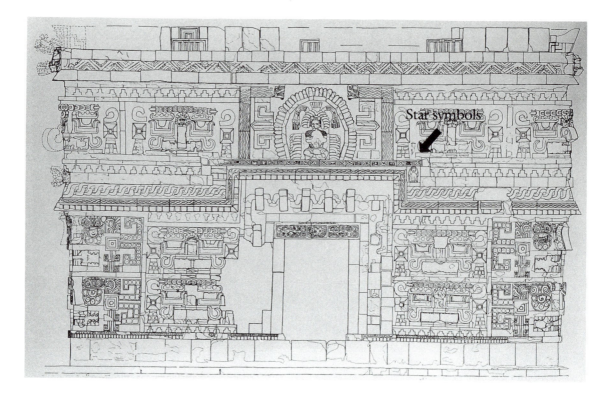

Figure 10.5. East wing of the Monjas complex at Chichén Itzá. From *Las Monjas* by John S. Bolles. Copyright © 1977 by the University of Oklahoma Press.

Scorpio. At any rate, it is clear from the dictionaries that at least three animals were envisioned in the night sky: the turtle, the rattlesnake, and the scorpion. All three of these are in the Paris Codex constellation pages; in fact, they lie side by side on page 24 (Fig. 10.1), forming a sequence (from right to left): rattlesnake, turtle, scorpion.

Images from Bonampak (Miller 1986:48, Plates 16, 19) lend powerful support to the notion of constellations as animals; a turtle and a pair of copulating peccaries are highlighted by star symbols (Fig. 10.6). The Bonampak pictures are important because clusters of stars, not just single stars, dot the animal figures. Clusters of stars strongly suggest constellations. With Bonampak as a model, the Monjas frieze can be reinterpreted. The star signs with the animals do not say, as Seler thought, that Venus was in a particular constellation, but that the animals themselves *are* constellations.

Kelley has reexamined the Monjas-Paris connection, found the matchup to be valid (though he changed some of Seler's animal identifications), and concluded that the case for a zodiac was still plausible, though not conclusive. Recent work by Bricker and Bricker (1992), however, shows that the Monjas frieze has been reconstructed and therefore is not in its original layout. Based on their review of the literature and an on-site inspection of the stonework, they convincingly argue that the Monjas "zodiac" has misled modern researchers and that it cannot be used to either confirm or refute the zodiac hypothesis for the Paris Codex (although, on other grounds, they are convinced that the Paris Codex does display a zodiac).

Herbert Spinden (1916; 1924:55–56) proposed a zodiac for the Paris Codex, matching the animal series on pages 23–24 with specific constellations in the European zodiac. He began in the top right corner of the Paris with the rattlesnake aligned with the Pleiades, followed by the turtle aligned with Gemini, though he suggested that the zodiac was used to mark the movement

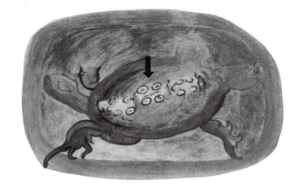

Figure 10.6. Constellation signs in the Bonampak murals (Miller 1986 : Plates 16, 19). *Left,* peccaries; *right,* turtle.

of the moon. Aveni (1980 : 201) also suggests a lunar function for the zodiac.

Kelley (1976 : 49), as mentioned above, has suggested that the Paris constellations are separated by 168-day intervals, that they represent constellations one-third to one-half of a sky apart, and that they represent successive zodiacal constellations but in the reverse order. Bricker and Bricker (1992) interpret adjacent animal figures as pairs of constellations, seen in the morning and evening sky, probably at sunrise. Based on their model, the Paris zodiac pages cover one-half of a year.

Without reviewing the complex arguments that Kelley and the Brickers present, and without discussing each point in those arguments, an alternative model can be put forward here that has as its strongest support the essence of simplicity. Following Spinden's (1924 : 55) lead, the thirteen constellations, laid out by the Maya scribe from top right to bottom left, correspond to thirteen successive constellations encircling the Maya sky. This model works, as shown below, both astronomically and ethnographically.

So far, two Maya star groups have been identified with known Western constellations: *Tsab,* the rattles of the rattlesnake, is the Pleiades (Barrera Vásquez 1980 : 849); and *Ac,* the turtle, is Orion (Lounsbury 1982 : 166–167). The Motul Dictionary (Martínez Hernández 1929 : 66) gives *ac ek* "turtle star" as three stars in the sign of Gemini, which with others make the form of a turtle. As Lounsbury explains, in the sixteenth century the "sign of Gemini" was not the constellation Gemini, but included the stars of Orion and much of Taurus. The three stars of the turtle in the Motul Dictionary are probably the same three stars seen on the Bonampak turtle (Fig. 10.6), namely, Orion's belt. In the night sky, Orion and the Pleiades appear next to each other, with the Pleiades to the observer's right. In the Paris Codex, the rattlesnake and the turtle also appear together, with the rattlesnake on the right. This one-to-one correspondence between the real night sky and the Paris Codex is very suggestive.

Recent ethnographic work in Yucatán adds tantalizing support to this model. John Sosa reports that in Yalcobá the "scorpion star" is a constellation of stars "from Orion to Sirius" (1985 : 431). In my own recent ethnographic fieldwork, southeast of Valladolid, I was told that the scorpion reached from the twin stars of Gemini all the way to Sirius, almost on the southern horizon. These two observations, Sosa's and my own, shatter the notion that the Maya scorpion constellation is necessarily the same as Scorpio in the Western tradition. Even though Redfield (1934 : 206) did report that *zinaan* "scorpion" was in fact Scorpio, and recent ethnography in Quintana Roo also equates the two (Nikolai Grube, personal communication, 1992), this may or may not be the result of modern Western influences. Modern researchers should not seek to match the Paris Codex constellations to the "signs of the zodiac" and certainly should not make the a priori assumption that the Maya scorpion is the Western Scorpio. The Paris Codex constellations are signs of the night, potent influences on earthly endeavors. They do not necessarily lie on the ecliptic, and they almost certainly do not correspond neatly with our own signs of the zodiac.

If the Maya scorpion includes the twin stars of the constellation Gemini, as Sosa's and my own fieldwork has shown, then the matchup of the Paris Codex constellations to the real night sky is strengthened. In the Paris Codex, the scorpion lies to the left of the turtle. In the night sky, Gemini also lies in that position, east of Orion. Together they form a succession of signs: Pleiades-Orion-Gemini, captured on paper by the ancient Maya priesthood as rattlesnake-turtle-scorpion. Amazingly, this same series figures prominently in the night skies of Momostenango. Barbara Tedlock reports: "During the dry half of the year, between harvest and planting (November through April), stellar risings and settings are observed and used in timing ritual events. Each of six such events, spaced from twenty to thirty days apart, singles out a particular star or constellation as *retal ak'ab* ('the sign of the night'). Thus in mid-November, the Pleiades rise near the sunrise position during evening twilight. . . . Other key stellar rise and set events occur in mid-December, with Orion; [and] in mid-January, with Gemini . . . " (Tedlock 1992: 182). The series of signs continues with Regulus (in Leo), the Big Dipper, and the Southern Cross. Of the six signs of the night recorded in Momostenango, only three lie within the zodiacal band; yet they are perceived by the modern Maya to rise in sequence, "twenty to thirty days apart," a succession like the animal constellations in the Paris Codex.

In Figure 10.7, the night sky is displayed with the Maya animal figures evenly spaced at thirteen intervals, with the rattlesnake-Pleiades, turtle-Orion, and scorpion-Gemini matchups tying the systems together. Perhaps future documentary and ethnographic research can confirm or refute this model, identifying certain star clusters as animal figures that match or do not match the layout presented here. According to this model, the constellation Leo would be associated with a kind of bird, the bird lying next in

line after the scorpion on the Paris Codex pages. Thompson (1950:116) briefly mentions that a Maya informant once called Orion *ac* "turtle," a piece of ethnographic data that Lounsbury (1982: 166–167) later used as part of his argument equating the turtle constellation with Orion. It is quite likely that such star lore still survives with certain ritual specialists in the forests of Yucatán today. While Tedlock has extracted native star knowledge from her fieldwork in Guatemala, Yucatán awaits the skilful ethnographer with the right questions and the facility to hear and record the answers.

USING THE CODEX SIGNS OF THE NIGHT

A Maya priest gazing from atop a pyramid watches the eastern horizon as the sun sets behind him in the west. As the sky darkens, a constellation appears, perhaps the rattlesnake, hovering over the horizon. As twilight turns to darkness, the rattlesnake journeys upward, reaching its highest point at midnight. Then it slowly descends to the western horizon, where it disappears as the new day dawns in the east. Night after night the rattlesnake reigns over the darkened land, and the priest in his wisdom fuses the omen of the rattlesnake with all other prognostications affecting those days and nights. But gradually, day after day, the rattlesnake is higher and higher in the sky as the sun sets, and there is a greater distance between the rattlesnake and eastern horizon. Soon the first faint stars of the sea turtle appear below the rattlesnake. As the rattlesnake passes upward, the great sea turtle takes its place, hovering over the horizon as darkness descends. In the twilight stillness it is threatening, proclaiming its power over the earth. The omen changes and the nights of the rattlesnake become the nights of the sea turtle. They are charged with new meaning.

The sea turtle is gradually replaced by the scorpion, then the bird, then the sea creature, and so on through the thirteen signs of the night until a year has passed, when once again gazing eastward, Ah Kin, the sun priest, beholds the awesome rattlesnake haunting the skies, poised for attack as nighttime falls.

THE 1,820-DAY ROUND

All Maya calendrical and celestial computations have at their core the magical *tsolkin,* the 260-day essence of cosmic interpretation. And so the procession of wondrous constellations is fused with the *tsolkin* count. Appearing in the center of pages 23 and 24, surrounded by constellations above and below, lies the formula counting the star's passage through the heavens (the missing portions can be reconstructed with confidence, based on the regularity of the visible parts [Fig. 10.1]).

The table begins at the top right corner. One reads to the left along the top row to the end, then goes to the far right in the second row, reads left to the end, goes to the far right in the third row, and so on to finish at the far bottom left. From that point, one moves back to the top right and the cycle continues. Each entry in this table is a day in the *tsolkin,* and each interval between entries is 28 days. One row across is 364 days, and five rows makes 1,820 days, or seven complete *tsolkins.* The Maya priest knew it took a full year for the rattlesnake to reappear in the same position at sunset. If there were thirteen constellations more or less evenly spaced across the sky, the average time for one constellation to replace another, relative to the horizon at sunset, would be 28 days ($365 \div 13 = 28.08$).

Suppose a Maya lord wanted to organize a hunting party to get provisions for an upcoming public feast. He would go to the Ah Kin, the sun priest, for counsel. The Ah Kin would first consult his hunting almanacs to find the propitious days; for the sake of argument, suppose that 3 Kan was the best day to go. But then, in order to deepen his understanding, he would consult the pages with the signs of the night to see which constellation was influencing 3 Kan. He would find 3 Kan in the top row, third from the right. Along the skyband, the third position from the right would be the sea turtle, so he would know which constellation would be influencing the days around 3 Kan. The omen of the sea turtle would be included in the priest's reckonings and duly conveyed to the inquiring lord. Perhaps he would call for a special ritual. If the trip was near

the day 2 Eb (ninth from the right, top row), the ninth constellation, the bat, would be affecting the hunting party. The following year, the priest would use the second row in the table, and in the third year, the third row, until five years had passed; then he could use the top row again to align *tsolkin* dates with signs of the night.

CORRECTION NUMBERS

As the Maya priest moved through the 1,820-day table, matching *tsolkin* dates with the constellations, he would begin to notice the stars slowly shifting out of step with the *tsolkin.* The first year he used the table, the complete sea turtle would be visible above the horizon on 3 Kan. After five years, when he returned to the top row in the table, he would notice that only about three-quarters of the turtle would be visible on 3 Kan. When using the top row again in the tenth year, the turtle would be only about half visible. He would know it was necessary to make some adjustments soon or the *tsolkin* dates would no longer match the constellations. If he used the table another complete time, only a fourth of the turtle would be visible on 3 Kan. This slippage, or falling out of sync, was a result of the table being based on multiples of 364 days, while the constellations themselves reappeared in the same position, relative to the horizon at sunset, every $365\frac{1}{4}$ days.

To adjust the *tsolkin* table to realign his readings, he would carefully move all the *tsolkin* dates forward twenty days to bring them back into alignment with the constellations. He would do this by changing the bar-and-dot coefficients in the columns. Below the column of threes (3 Kan, 3 Lamat, 3 Eb, 3 Cib, and 3 Ahau) he would draw two bars, signifying the number ten, in green paint (Fig. 10.1). Now 3 Kan would be read 10 Kan, a point twenty days forward in the *tsolkin.* Likewise, 3 Lamat would be 10 Lamat, 3 Eb would be 10 Eb, and so on. He would write his green adjustment numbers in each column, either above or below, depending on available space, and when he was through, the entire table would have been moved forward twenty days. The sacred *tsolkin* dates would once again be aligned

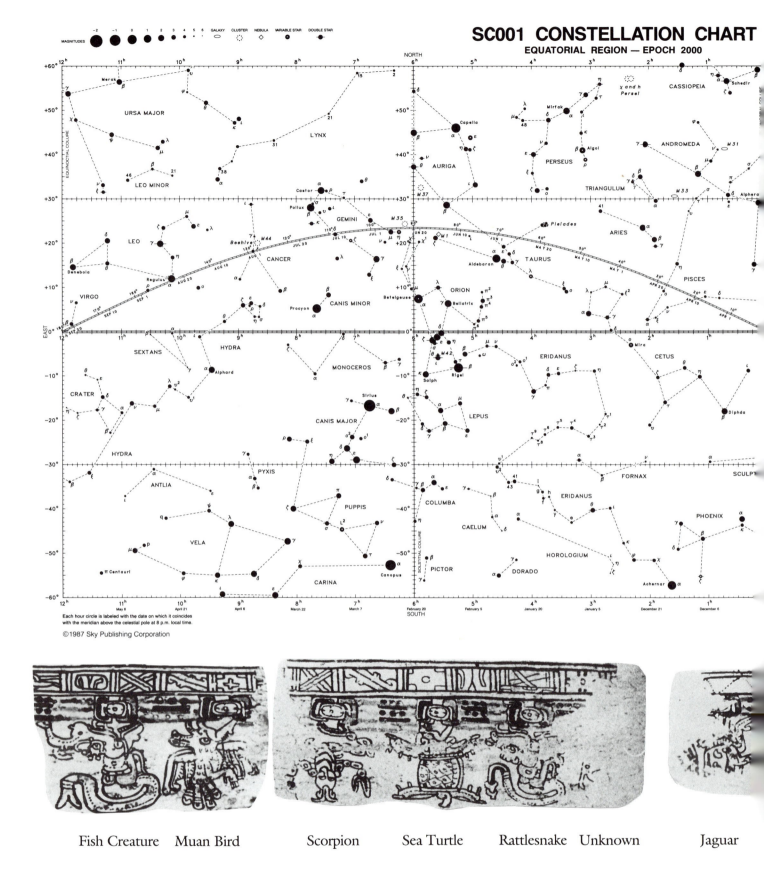

Fish Creature   Muan Bird   Scorpion   Sea Turtle   Rattlesnake   Unknown   Jaguar

Figure 10.7. A constellation chart (Sky Publishing Corporation 1980) aligned with the Paris constellations. The Pleiades and Orion are aligned with the rattlesnake and the turtle, which in turn causes Gemini to match up with the scorpion, an alignment recently confirmed ethnographically in Yucatán.

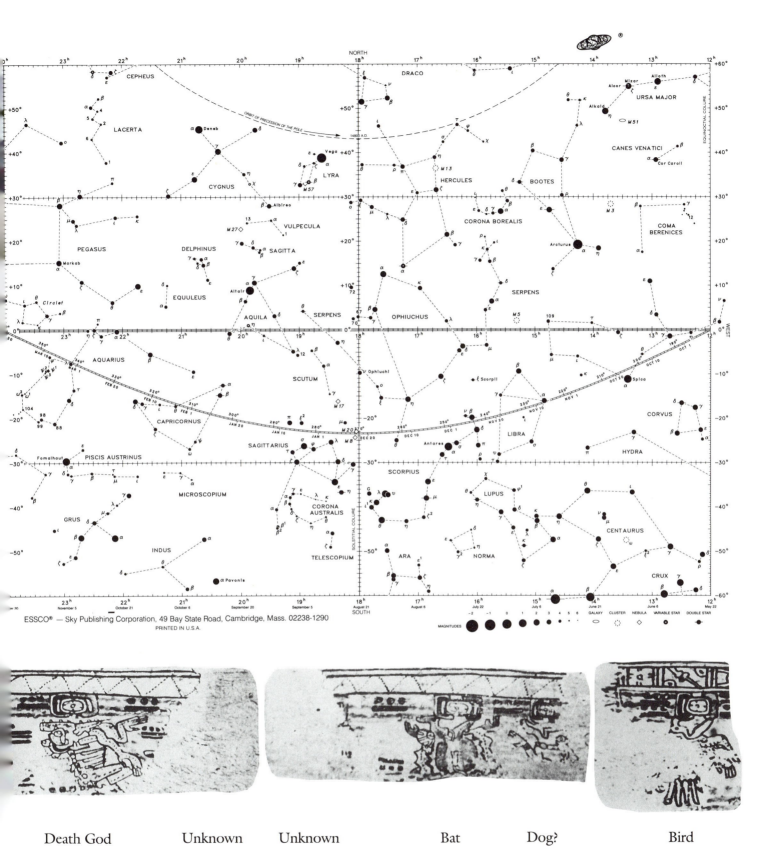

ESSCO® — Sky Publishing Corporation, 49 Bay State Road, Cambridge, Mass. 02238-1290

PRINTED IN U.S.A.

Death God   Unknown   Unknown   Bat   Dog?   Bird

with the mighty constellations. On 10 Kan (where the original table read 3 Kan) the great sea turtle would once again rule over the night. The Paris signs of the night, with the one correction forward, would be useful to a Maya priest for twenty or thirty years, perhaps the average length of one priest's tenure.

Seler (1904 : 21) first proposed that the green numbers (Fig. 10.1) in the day-sign table were used to add twenty days to the day signs, but only now do we understand why twenty days were added (a discovery also made by Dieter Dütting [1988] and the team of Richard Johnson and Michel Quenon from the Texas Maya Workshops in 1992). There are two lines of evidence that the numbers were added after the original codex was painted: the numbers are squeezed into available space because no room was allowed for them in the original layout, and the numbers' particular shade of blue-green is found nowhere else in the codex (Gates 1910 : 34).

THE 364-DAY TABLE

There is a secondary function for the day signs on pages 23 and 24. Even without reference to the signs of the night and without considering the omens or the influences of the constellations, the table still serves as a useful tool for the practicing Maya priest. It can serve as a calculating table for finding days in the *tsolkin,* forward or backward in time. Eric Thompson (1942) successfully demonstrated how a Maya calendar specialist could use counts of 364 days to make many kinds of calculations. In the Dresden codex there are no less than three sections dealing with multiples of 364. Here in the Paris Codex the table is a simple tool by which a specialist could see and count positions in the *tsolkin.* The key to its success is that five times 364 equals exactly seven *tsolkins.* Picking any column in the day-sign table, one can move down the column by increments of 364 days and move horizontally to the left by increments of 28 days. The reverse direction moves one backward in time. This table allows the priest to see into the past or the future and determine where days fall in *tsolkins* far removed in time.

SUMMARY

The signs of the night of the Paris Codex present a visual tableau of Maya constellations that were yet another class of spirit beings—forces in the sky that influenced humans on the ground. The constellations that encircled the night sky were manifested on paper, in the priest's sacred codex, in a simple right-to-left pattern that matched the layout of the sky itself. As with all other Maya spirit influences, for the priest to foretell the future in a way that was functional and useful, prediction was tied to the *tsolkin,* that most sacred of all cycles, the never-ending round of 260 days.

Conclusion

A brief review of the preceding chapters points out the numerous levels on which a Maya book works. The *katun* pages display the *katun* lords interacting with the real-world priests of political and geographical space. Other *katun* lords, not pictured, are listed in the succession statements that initiate the text of each page. The Lord of the Katun is displaying his badge of authority, the God K head, symbolized in the script as a smoking head with an Akbal infix, the final phrase of the succession text. Following the introductory list are mostly undeciphered writings that have a historical component. They are texts with *"tun*-Ahau*"* statements—numbered *tuns* and *uinals* followed by numbered Ahaus naming the *katun*—the Yucatecan method of specifying historical dates both on monuments and in the colonial books of Chilam Balam. Above the *katun* pictorial scenes are texts full of omens and prophecies, also with numbered *tuns* and *uinals*.

Above the *katun* scenes lie the *tun-uinal* prophecies. The numbered Ahaus, reading across, provide a count of *tuns* accompanied by the pictures of gods on *tun* signs with brief hieroglyphic texts above. These provide the priest with the omens for the *tuns*. Reading the Ahau signs downward, from top to bottom, provides *uinal* intervals, a form of calendar reading that carries through to the Colonial Period.

The God C pages are a form of almanac presentation not found in the other codices but sharing much in common with certain Chac almanacs from the Dresden Codex. The texts begin *aan ku* "there is God C," followed by various manifestations of this omnipresent force. Between each scene, columns of colored bars and dots and two forms of "twenty" give prescriptions for properly

counted ritual offerings. Below the God C almanacs lie other, more standard almanacs dealing with Chac and weather.

The yearbearer pages lay out a fifty-two-year sequence of yearbearers, days that begin the Maya 365-day years. The omens for the years, mostly expressed as conditions of the Maize God, allow the priest to color his readings with broad predictions of abundance and sustenance or famine and death.

The day-sign page presents a tableau of abbreviated almanacs, both the 260-day and the 520-day variety. Each column is like the lead column in an almanac but without the following *t'ols*. They are linked by green skycords to the sun sign in a field of rain, yet another way for the Maya priest to foretell the weather.

The spirit-world pages display an arrangement of spirit forces, both from the heavens and the underworld. The Pauahtuns reign in the sky while death gods rule below. Attacking serpents emanate from the hollow eyes of death itself.

Finally, the constellation pages allow the priest to interweave yet another level of spirit forces, the signs of the night. Heavenly constellations, in the form of animals, rule in the sky during successive periods of 28 days. The influence of these powers is tied to the never-ending 260-day *tsolkin* in a table of five lines of 364 days each. Correction numbers allow the priest to readjust the *tsolkin* counts as they gradually fall out of alignment with the stars.

To the native priest peering into the Paris Codex, the myriad forces of the spirit world were arranged and organized on the pages before him. The awesome interweaving of cycles within cycles became comprehensible and predictable. The *katuns, tuns, uinals, kins, tsolkins,* yearbearers, and constellations all extended their omens over the Maya people. The priest, with his books, could see them, read them, and interpret them. The fantastic invisible world became perceivable as the great cosmological mysteries were reduced to understandable formulae. Modern researchers may peer into these very same pages and glimpse the magical Maya world, where a multitude of forces merge into a system that is harmonious and complete.

Appendix

European Writing in the Paris Codex
by Grant D. Jones

On pages 9, 15, 16, and 19 of the Paris Codex there are traces of Spanish writing. Because the study of these notations has just begun, the findings are tentative. Much of the ink has faded away, and the copies I am working with are inferior. Nonetheless, some highly probable conclusions may be proffered at this time.

At least one person (but probably two or three) who was literate in Spanish has written what appear to be glosses of Maya hieroglyphs, Spanish translations, and possibly descriptive phrases (the nature of which are unclear) in Spanish. The writer either knew how to read glyphs or worked with an informant who did. Based on paleographic comparisons with other documents, the date of the writing appears to be from the mid- to late- seventeenth century to no later than the mid-eighteenth century.

These points, taken together, lead to a fascinating possibility. Where is it documented in the historical literature that there were writers of Spanish who could translate glyphs around 1700? Although such a situation could have occurred in numerous locations throughout Yucatán, there is only one place where it is firmly documented. That place is among the Itza Maya of Tah Itza (Tayasal, also known as Noh Peten "Big Island")

in the 1690s. Codices were noted by Fray Andrés de Avendaño y Loyola (1987) in 1696, when the Itza still possessed them, and there is clear evidence that Ursua had one or more of them in his possession. He wrote to the king on July 30, 1697:

> The genealogy of the king's native lord[ship] was found in his house, with painting and design that is truly singular and admirable, made of beaten bark from trees, and I am still waiting for [an explanation of] the prophecies from it, which I have solicited. According to Don Martín Chan only he [the king] and his priest are able to explain them. If I obtain [this explanation], I will send it, although due to the disruptive obstinacy of the priest and dishonesty of the [*sic*] Canek, I may find myself unable to do this. (Ursua y Arismendi 1697)

Ursua could be describing the Paris Codex here. The succession of figures on thrones in the codex could certainly be interpreted as a "genealogy." Two Yucatecan clergymen, as part of a sworn declaration on April 10, 1699, referred to "books made of tree-bark, and their pages of *betun* [referring to the limestone coating?], in which they

---

Author's note: At the conclusion of writing the text of the present book, I received this information from Grant D. Jones, who has begun a study of the faint traces of European writing that appear on several pages of the Paris Codex. Rather

than incorporating Grant's findings into the book, I am adding them here as an appendix. The implications of Grant's discoveries are tantalizing, to say the least.

kept their prophecies, which are presently in the possession of Señor Don Martín de Ursua" (Morales and Mora 1699).

My efforts to decipher the handwriting follow.

Page 9

The writing lies between the two Ahau signs in the upper register. There is a letter *m* with a flourish before it, probably the letter *o*. The *m* is followed by letters that could be *isi, esi, ese, ye,* or *yi*. This is followed by what appears to be *ahhau*. The *ahhau* is not certain, but it makes sense in light of the Ahau signs above and below it.

Page 15

Line 1. The writing crosses a cluster of dots to the right of the God C figure with the three maize tamale offerings. It appears to begin with the letter *d* and end with *vn (un)*. The letters in between are too faded to read clearly, but following the *d* is the beginning of a slanted letter with a loop at the top, followed by what appears to be an *a*. I see what may be *d- ka-un,* possibly rendering *de katun.*

Line 2. The writing lies between the large bar-and-dot seven and the *kal* ("twenty") sign below it. It possibly reads *juella,* which, modernized as *huella,* would mean "path" or "track." Alternatively, it might be *juessa,* modernized as *huessa,* "grave" or "tomb."

Line 3. The writing begins on or before the face below the seated God C, crosses the cross-hatched glyph to the right, and goes at least as far as the *kal* glyph for "twenty" to its right. On the face is clearly *u uuc,* translated "its seven." It appears set off from the other glosses and may be written in another hand. This could refer to the

bar-and-dot seven to its right. *U uuc* is followed by what may be *n* or *vi*. Inside the next glyph appears *pa,* followed by what may be an *l*. The cross-hatched glyph, in Mayan, is phonetic *pa.* Between this and the next glyph may be *lu*. There is writing across the right side of the *kal* glyph, ending in what appears to be a large zero ("o"). Could this be part of the number twenty, with the "two" hidden behind the glyph?

Page 16

There is writing on the *Yaxche* (ceiba) tree on which God C is seated, but nothing can be made out at this time.

Page 19

Line 1. Across the top bar of the bar-and-dot number thirteen is apparently the word *dia,* preceded by a two-letter word ending in *a,* but it cannot grammatically be *la.* Following *dia* seems to be a *u* followed by two vertical lines and a superscript *a.* I suspect this is *ult* for *ultima,* rendering *?a dia ult* "the last day."

Line 2. Above the four dots over the Ben sign below the one just discussed is clearly *dia de* and a third word, which perhaps starts with *c.* Could this be *cuch* "yearbearer" or perhaps *cuatro* "four"? It is followed by a letter with a downward loop (not *q*) and a second illegible letter.

The foregoing summarizes my preliminary study of the Spanish writing in the Paris Codex. Ultraviolet light photography of the original manuscript would bring out the faded ink and clear up many mysteries. I can only hope that this humble beginning will stimulate more intensive investigations into this potentially very fruitful line of research.

Bibliography

Anders, Ferdinand
  1968   *Codex Peresianus (Codex Paris), Bibliothèque Nacionale, Paris: Einleitung und Summary.* Graz, Austria: Akademische Druck- und Verlagsanstalt. [Accompanies boxed facsimile of Paris Codex 1968.]

Anderson, Donald M.
  1969   *The Art of Written Forms: The Theory and Practice of Calligraphy.* New York: Holt, Rinehart and Winston.

Aubin, Joseph Marius Alexis
  1849   *Mémoire sur la peinture didactique et l'écriture figurative des anciens Mexicains.* Paris: Paul Dupont.

Avendaño y Loyola, Fray Andrés de
  1987   *Relation of Two Trips to Peten: Made for the Conversion of the Heathen Ytzaex and Cehaches.* Translated by Charles P. Bowditch and Guillermo Rivera. Edited by Frank Comparato. Culver City, Calif: Labyrinthos.

Aveni, Anthony F.
  1980   *Skywatchers of Ancient Mexico.* Austin: University of Texas Press.

Baeza, Bartolomé del Granado
  1845   Los indios de Yucatán. *Registro Yucateco* 1: 165–178. [Originally published in 1813 by Castillo y Compañía in Mérida.]

Barrera Vásquez, Alfredo
  1948   *El libro de los libros de Chilam Balam.* Mexico City: Fondo de Cultura Económica.
  1976   *El folklore de Yucatán.* Ediciones del Gobierno del Estado. Mérida: Talleres Gráficos y Editorial "Zamna." [Spanish translation of Brinton 1883 with notes; originally published in 1937, Publication 3, Museo Arqueología de Yucatán, Mérida.]
  1980   *Diccionario Maya Cordemex, Maya-Español, Español-Maya.* Mérida: Ediciones Cordemex.

Barrera Vásquez, Alfredo, and Sylvanus Morley

1949   *The Maya Chronicles.* Contributions to American Anthropology and History, no. 48. Publication 585. Washington, D.C.: Carnegie Institution of Washington.

Beltran de Santa Rosa María, Fray R. P.
  1746   *Arte de el idioma Maya reducído a succintas* [sic] *reglas, y semilexicon yucateco.* Mexico City: La Viuda de D. Joseph Bernardo de Hogal.

Benson, Elizabeth P.
  1976   Ritual Cloth and Palenque Kings. In *The Art, Iconography, and Dynastic History of Palenque, Part III.* Proceedings of the Segunda Mesa Redonda de Palenque. Edited by Merle Green Robertson, pp. 45–58. Pebble Beach, Calif.: Robert Louis Stevenson School, Pre-Columbian Art Research.

Bolles, John
  1977   *Las Monjas.* Norman: University of Oklahoma Press.

Bowditch, Charles P.
  1939   *Gesammelte Abhandlungen zur amerikanishen Sprach- und Alterthumskunde: Unpublished English Translations of German Papers in the Above Work Made under the Supervision of Charles P. Bowditch.* 5 vols. Cambridge, Mass.: Carnegie Institution of Washington.

Brasseur de Bourbourg, Charles Etienne
  1852   Des Antiquités Mexicaines. À propos du mémoire 1853 sur la peinture Didactique . . . por M. J. A. Aubin. *Revue Archéologique* 9 (2): 408–421.
  1857–1859   *Histoire des nations civilisées du Mexique et de l'Amerique-Centrale durant les siècles antérieurs à Christophe Colomb.* 4 vols. Paris.
  1867   *Archives de la Commission Scientifique du Mexique.* Vol. 2. Paris: Ministere de l'Instruction Publique.
  1870   *Manuscrit Troano. Études sur le système graphique et la langue des Mayas.* 2 vols. Paris: Imprimerie Imperial.

1871   *Bibliothèque Mexico-Guatemalienne précédée d'un coup d'oeil sur les études Americaines . . .* Paris: Maisonneuve & Cie.

Bricker, Harvey M., and Victoria R. Bricker

1983   Classic Maya Prediction of Solar Eclipses. *Current Anthropology* 24 (1): 1–23.

1992   Zodiacal References in the Maya Codices. In *The Sky in Mayan Literature.* Edited by Anthony Aveni, pp. 148–183. New York: Oxford University Press.

Forthcoming   See 1992.

Brinton, Daniel G.

1883   The Folklore of Yucatán. *Folklore Journal* 1: 244–256.

1895   *A Primer of Mayan Hieroglyphs.* University of Pennsylvania Series in Philology, Literature, and Archaeology, vol. 3, no. 2. Philadelphia: University of Pennsylvania.

Burland, Cottie A.

1947   A 360-Day Count in a Mexican Codex. *Man* 47:106–108.

1966   *Codex Laud.* Facsimile edition. Introduction by Cottie A. Burland. Codices Selecti, Vol. 11. Graz, Austria: Akademische Druck- und Verlagsanstalt.

Carlson, John B.

1988   Skyband Representations in Classic Maya Vase Painting. In *Maya Iconography.* Edited by Elizabeth P. Benson and Gillett G. Griffin, pp. 277–293. Princeton, N.J.: Princeton University Press.

1989   God C. Paper presented at the Septima Mesa Redonda, Palenque, Mexico, June 1989.

Carlson, John B., and Linda C. Landis

1985   Bands, Bicephalic Dragons, and Other Beasts: The Skyband in Maya Art and Iconography. In *Fourth Palenque Round Table, 1980.* Vol. 6. Edited by Merle Greene Robertson (General Editor) and Elizabeth P. Benson (Volume Editor), pp. 115–140. San Francisco: Pre-Columbian Art Research Institute.

Chamberlain, Robert S.

1948   *The Conquest and Colonization of Yucatán: 1517–1550.* Carnegie Institution of Washington Publication 582. Washington, D.C.: Carnegie Institution of Washington.

Chase, Diane

1985   Between Earth and Sky: Idols, Images, and Postclassic Cosmology. In *Fifth Palenque Round Table, 1983.* Vol. 7. Edited by Merle Greene Robertson (General Editor) and Virginia M. Fields (Volume Editor), pp. 223–

233. San Francisco: Pre-Columbian Art Research Institute.

Ciudad Real, Antonio de

1984   *Calepino Maya de Motul.* Edición de Rene Acuna. Mexico City: Instituto de Investigaciones Filológicas, Universidad Nacional Autónoma de México.

Closs, Michael P.

1983   Were the Ancient Maya Aware of the Precession of the Equinoxes? *Archaeoastronomy* 6 (1–4): 164–171.

1989   Cognitive Aspects of Ancient Maya Eclipse Theory. In *World Archaeoastronomy: Selected Papers from the Second Oxford International Conference on Archaeoastronomy Held at Mérida, Yucatán, Mexico, 13–17 January 1986.* Edited by Anthony Aveni, pp. 389–415. Cambridge: Cambridge University Press.

Códice Pérez

ca. 1875   *Chilam Balam (Libro sagrado o profético).* Ms. copied by Carillo y Ancona. Original in the Princeton Collection of Western Americana, Princeton University Library, Princeton, N.J.; photographic reproduction at the Center for Maya Research, Washington, D.C.

Coe, Michael D.

1973   *The Maya Scribe and His World.* New York: Grolier Club.

1977   Supernatural Patrons of Maya Scribes and Artists. In *Social Process in Maya Prehistory.* Edited by Norman Hammond, pp. 327–347. New York: Academic Press.

1989   *The Royal Fifth: Earliest Notices of Maya Writing.* Research Reports on Ancient Maya Writing no. 28. Washington, D.C.: Center for Maya Research.

Commission Scientifique du Mexique

See Paris Codex 1864

Cospi, Codex

See Nowotny 1968

Craine, Eugene R., and Reginald C. Reindorp

1979   *The Codex Pérez and the Book of Chilam Balam of Maní.* Translated and edited by Eugene R. Craine and Reginald C. Reindorp. Norman: University of Oklahoma Press.

Duruy, S. E. M.

See Paris Codex 1864

Dütting, Dieter, and Matthias Schramm

1988   The Sidereal Period of the Moon in Maya Calendrical Astronomy. *Tribus,* no. 37:139–163. Stuttgart: Linden-Museum Stuttgart Staatliches Museum für Völkerkunde.

Edmonson, Munro S.

1982 *The Ancient Future of the Itza: The Book of Chilam Balam of Tizimin.* Translated and annotated by Munro S. Edmonson. Austin: University of Texas Press.

Fash, William L., Jr.

1989 The Sculptural Façade of Structure 9N–82: Content, Form, and Significance. In *The House of the Bacabs, Copan, Honduras.* Edited by David Webster, pp. 41–72. Studies in Pre-Columbian Art and Archaeology, no. 29. Washington, D.C.: Dumbarton Oaks.

1991 *Scribes, Warriors, and Kings: The City of Copán and the Ancient Maya.* New York: Thames and Hudson.

Fejervary-Mayer, Codex

1971 *Codex Fejervary-Mayer.* 12014 M, City of Liverpool Museums. Facsimile edition. Introduction by C. A. Burland. Graz, Austria: Akademische Druck- und Verlagsanstalt.

Förstemann, Ernst

1903 *Commentary on the Paris Maya Manuscript (Codex Peresianus).* Danzig: L. Sauniers Bookstore.

1906 *Commentary on the Maya Manuscript in the Royal Public Library of Dresden.* Papers of the Peabody Museum of American Archaeology and Ethnology, Harvard University, vol. 4, no. 2. Cambridge: Peabody Museum.

Fox, James A., and John S. Justeson

1984 Polyvalence in Mayan Hieroglyphic Writing. In *Phoneticism in Mayan Hieroglyphic Writing.* Edited by John S. Justeson and Lyle Campbell, pp. 17–76. Publication no. 9. Albany: Institute for Mesoamerican Studies, State University of New York at Albany.

Gann, Thomas W. F.

1900 *Mounds in Northern Honduras.* Bureau of American Ethnology Nineteenth Annual Report to the Secretary of the Smithsonian Institution, 1897–1898. Washington, D.C.: Government Printing Office.

1917 The Chachac, or Rain Ceremony, as Practised by the Maya of Southern Yucatán and Northern British Honduras. In *Proceedings of the Nineteenth International Congress of Americanists.* Edited by F. W. Hodge, pp. 409–418. Washington, D.C.

1918 *The Maya Indians of Southern Yucatán and Northern British Honduras.* Bureau of American Ethnology Bulletin, no. 64. Washington, D.C.: Government Printing Office.

Gates, William Edmund

1909 *Codex Pérez Maya-Tzental. Redrawn and slightly restored, and with the coloring as it originally stood, so far as possible, given on a new and minute examination of the codex itself. Mounted in the form of the original. Accompanied by a reproduction of the 1864 photographs; also by the entire text of the glyphs, unemended but with some restorations, printed from type, and arranged in parallel columns for convenience of study and comparison, and with a set of blank cards, corresponding to the printed text as arranged and numbered.* Boxed edition. [Point Loma, Calif.]

1910 *Commentary upon the Maya-Tzental Pérez Codex with a Concluding Note upon the Linguistic Problem of the Maya Glyphs.* Papers of the Peabody Museum of Archaeology and Ethnology, Harvard University, vol. 6, no. 2. Cambridge: Peabody Museum.

Glass, John B.

1975a A Census of Native Middle American Pictorial Manuscripts. In *Handbook of Middle American Indians.* Vol. 14. Edited by Robert Wauchope (General Editor), Howard F. Cline (Volume Editor), Charles Gibson, and H. B. Nicholson (Associate Volume Editors), pp. 81–253. Austin: University of Texas Press.

1975b Annotated References. In *Handbook of Middle American Indians.* Vol. 15. Edited by Robert Wauchope (General Editor), Howard F. Cline (Volume Editor), Charles Gibson, and H. B. Nicholson (Associated Volume Editors), pp. 537–724. Austin: University of Texas Press.

Gordon, George B.

1913 *The Book of Chilam Balam of Chumayel.* Photographic facsimile. Introduction by G. B. Gordon. University of Pennsylvania Museum Anthropological Publications, vol. 5. Philadelphia: University of Pennsylvania Museum.

Graham, Ian

1978 *Corpus of Maya Hieroglyphic Inscriptions.* Vol. 2, part 2. Cambridge: Peabody Museum of Archaeology and Ethnology. Harvard University.

Hellmuth, Nicholas M.

1987 *Monster und Menschen in der Maya-Kunst.* Graz, Austria: Akademische Druck- und Verlagsanstalt.

Justeson, John

1989　Ancient Maya Ethnoastronomy: An Overview of Hieroglyphic Sources. In *World Archaeoastronomy: Selected Papers from the Second Oxford International Conference on Archaeoastronomy Held at Mérida, Yucatán, Mexico, 13–17 January 1986*. Edited by Anthony Aveni, pp. 76–129. Cambridge: Cambridge University Press.

Kelley, David H.

1976　*Deciphering the Maya Script*. Austin: University of Texas Press.

Kidder, Alfred V.

1937　*Notes on the Ruins of San Agustín Acasaguastlan, Guatemala*. Contributions to American Archaeology, no. 15. Washington, D.C.: Carnegie Institution of Washington. [Issued November 1935.]

Kingsborough, Edward King

1829–1848　*Antiquities of Mexico, Comprising Facsimiles of Ancient Mexican Paintings and Hieroglyphics, Preserved in the Royal Libraries of Paris, Berlin, and Dresden; in the Imperial Library of Vienna; in the Vatican Library; in the Borgian Museum at Rome; in the Library of the Institute at Bologna; and in the Bodlein Library at Oxford. Together with the Monuments of New Spain, by M. Dupaix; with their Respective Scales of Measurement and Accompanying Descriptions. The whole illustrated by Many Valuable Inedited Manuscripts, by Augustine Aglio*. 9 vols. London: James Moynes [vols. 1–7]; and London: Colnagi, Son and Co. [vols. 8 and 9].

Klein, Cecelia

1982　Woven Heaven, Tangled Earth: A Weaver's Paradigm of the Mesoamerican Cosmos. In *Ethnoastronomy and Archaeoastronomy in the American Tropics*. Annals of the New York Academy of Sciences, vol. 385. New York: New York Academy of Sciences.

Knorozov, Yuri V.

1963　*Pis'mennost' Indeitsev Maiia*. Moscow: Institut Etnografi Akademi Nauk.

1982　*Maya Hieroglyphic Codices*. Translated from the Russian by Sophie D. Coe. Publication 8. Albany: Institute for Mesoamerican Studies, State University of New York at Albany.

Landa, Diego de

[1566]　*Relación de las cosas de Yucatán sacada de lo que escrivio el padre fray Diego de Landa de la orden de Sto. Francisco*. Original in Real Academia de la Historia, Madrid, Spain. Photographic reproduction at Center for Maya Research, Washington, D.C.

Leclerq, Charles

1867　*Bibliotheca Americana: Catalogue raisonné d'une très-precieuse collection de livres anciens et modernes sur l'Amériques et les Philippines*. Paris: Maisonneuve et Cie.

1878　*Bibliotheca Americana. Histoire, géographie, voyages, archéologie et linguistique des deux Amériques et des îles Philippines*. Paris: Maisonneuve et Cie.

Lee, Thomas A.

1985　*Los códices Mayas. Introducción y bibliografía*. San Cristóbal de las Casas: Universidad Autónoma de Chiapas. [Accompanies color reproductions of the four known Maya codices.]

Le Rider, Georges

1976　*Aztlán, terre des Aztéques: Images d'un noveau monde*. Paris: Bibliothèque Nacionale. [Exhibition catalogue.]

Lipp, Frank Joseph

1991　*The Mixe of Oaxaca: Religion, Ritual, and Healing*. Austin: University of Texas Press.

Lombardo de Ruíz, Sonia, Alfredo Barrera Rubio, Martine Fettweis-Vienot, and Ruben Maldonado Cárdenas

1987　*La pintura mural Maya en Quintana Roo*. Colección Fuentes, Instituto Nacional de Antropología e Historia, Gobierno del Estado de Quintana Roo. Mexico City: Offset Setenta.

Lounsbury, Floyd G.

1978　Maya Numeration, Computation, and Calendrical Astronomy. *Dictionary of Scientific Biography* 15:759–818.

1982　Astronomical Knowledge and Its Uses at Bonampak, Mexico. In *Archaeoastronomy in the New World*. Edited by Anthony Aveni, pp. 143–168. Cambridge: Cambridge University Press.

Love, Bruce

1986　Yucatec Maya Ritual: A Diachronic Perspective. Ph.D. diss., University of California, Los Angeles.

1987　*Glyph T93 and Maya "Hand-scattering" Events*. Research Reports on Ancient Maya Writing, no. 5. Washington, D.C.: Center for Maya Research.

1989　Yucatec Maya Sacred Bread Through Time. In *Word and Image in Maya Culture: Explorations in Language, Writing, and Representation*. Edited by William Hanks and Don

Rice, pp. 336–350. Salt Lake City: University of Utah Press.

1991 A Text from the Dresden New Year Pages. In *Sixth Palenque Round Table: 1986*. Edited by Merle Greene Robertson (General Editor) and Virginia Fields (Volume Editor), pp. 293–302. Norman: University of Oklahoma Press.

1992 Divination and Prophecy in Yucatán. In *New Theories on the Ancient Maya* (University Museum Monograph 77). Edited by Elin C. Danien and Robert J. Sharer, pp. 205–212. Philadelphia: The University Museum, University of Pennsylvania.

Makemson, Maud W.

1943 *The Astronomical Tables of the Maya*. Contributions to American Anthropology and History no. 42. Carnegie Institution of Washington Publication 546. Washington, D.C.: Carnegie Institution of Washington.

Martínez Hernández, Juan

1929 *Diccionario de Motul, Maya-Español, atribuido a fray Antonio de Ciudad Real, y arte de lengua Maya por fray Juan Coronel*. Mérida: Compañía Tipográfica Yucateca.

Martínez Marín, Carlos

1961 *Codice Laud: Introducción, selección y notas*. Serie Investigaciones 5. Mexico City: Instituto Nacional de Antropología e Historia.

Martyr, Peter

1944 *Décadas del nuevo mundo*. Translated by D. Joaquin Torres Asensio; prologue by Luís A. Arocena. Buenos Aires: Editorial Bajel. [One of many editions of all eight of the "decades"; others are 1530 (Latin), 1555 (English), 1612 (English), 1912 (English translation by McNutt), etc.]

Mathews, Peter, and Linda Schele

1974 Lords of Palenque—Glyphic Evidence. In *Primera Mesa Redonda de Palenque, Part 1*. Edited by Merle Greene Robertson, pp. 63–76. Pebble Beach, Calif.: Robert Louis Stevenson School, Pre-Columbian Art Research.

Maudslay, Alfred P.

1889–1902 *Biologia Centrali-Americana; or, Contributions to the Knowledge of the Fauna and Flora of Mexico and Central America*. Vol. 4. Edited by F. Ducane Godman and Osbert Salvin. London: R. H. Porter and Dulau and Co.

Mayer, Karl Herbert

1980 *El Libro de Chilam Balam de Tizimin*. Facsimile edition. Introduction by Karl Herbert Mayer. Graz, Austria: Akademische Druck- und Verlagsanstalt.

1984 *Maya Monuments: Sculptures of Unknown Provenance in Middle America*. Berlin: Verlag Karl-Friedrich von Flemming.

1989 *Maya Monuments: Sculptures of Unknown Provenance, Supplement 2*. Berlin: Verlag von Flemming.

Means, Phillip A.

1917 *History of the Spanish Conquest of Yucatán and of the Itzás*. Papers of the Peabody Museum of American Archaeology and Ethnology, Harvard University, vol. 7. Cambridge: Peabody Museum.

Mengin, Ernst

1972 *Bocabulario de Mayathan: das Worterbuch der Yukatekischen Mayasprache*. [Vienna Dictionary.] Graz, Austria: Akademische Druck- und Verlagsanstalt.

Miller, Arthur G.

1982 *On the Edge of the Sea: Mural Painting at Tancah-Tulum, Quintana Roo, Mexico*. Washington, D.C.: Dumbarton Oaks.

Miller, Mary Ellen

1986 *The Murals of Bonampak*. Princeton, N.J.: Princeton University Press.

Morales, Pedro de, and José Francisco Martínez de Mora

1699 Parecer by Br. Pedro de Morales and José Francisco Martínez de Mora, 10 April, 1699. Guatemala 151A. Archivo General de Indias, Seville.

Morley, Sylvanus G.

1920 *The Inscriptions at Copan*. Carnegie Institution of Washington Publication 219. Washington, D.C.: Carnegie Institution of Washington.

Motul Dictionary

See Martínez Hernández

Nowotny, K. Anton

1961 *Tlacuilolli. Die Mexikanischen Bilderhandschriften, Stil und Inhalt, mit einem Katalog der Codex Borgia-Gruppe*. Monumenta Americana 3. Berlin: Gebr. Mann.

1968 *Codex Cospi*. Calendario Messicano 4093, Biblioteca Universitaria Bologna. Facsimile edition. Graz, Austria: Akademische Druck- und Verlagsanstalt.

Paris Codex, or Codex Peresianus, or Codex Paris, or "Pérez Codex"

1864 *Manuscrit dit Mexicain No. 2 de la Bibliothèque Impériale, photographié (sans réduction) par ordre de S. E. M. Duruy, Ministre de l'Instruc-*

tion publique, présidente de la Commission Scientifique du Mexique. Paris: Imprimerie Bonaventure et Ducessois, Imprimerie Photographique Benoist.

1887 See Rosny 1887

1888 See Rosny 1888

1933 See Willard 1933

1968 *Codex Peresianus (Codex Paris).* Codices Selecti, Phototypice Impressi, vol. 9. Graz, Austria: Akademische Druck- und Verlagsanstalt. [22-page facsimile boxed with Anders 1968.]

Pérez, José

1859a Note sur un ancien manuscrit americaine inédit. *Revue Orientale et Américaine* 1:35–39. [Illustrates one page of Paris Codex.]

1859b Note sur un manuscrit Yucatèque inédit. *Archives de la Société Américaine de France* 1: 29–32.

Pío Pérez, Juan

1898 Coordinación alfabética de las voces del idioma maya que se hallan en el arte y obra de Fr. Pedro Beltrán de Santa Rosa . . . Mérida.

Proskouriakoff, Tatiana

1952 *The Survival of the Maya Tun Count in Colonial Times: Notes on Pages 124–131 of the Codex Pérez and Pages 124–125 of the Kaua.* Notes on Middle American Archaeology and Ethnology, no. 112. Cambridge, Mass.: Carnegie Institution of Washington, Department of Archaeology.

1962 Civic and Religious Structures of Mayapan. In *Mayapan Yucatán Mexico,* pp. 87–164. Carnegie Institution of Washington Publication 619. Washington, D.C.: Carnegie Institution of Washington.

Proskouriakoff, Tatiana, and J. Eric S. Thompson

1947 *Maya Calendar Round Dates Such as 9 Ahau 17 Mol.* Notes on Middle American Archaeology and Ethnology, no. 79. Washington, D.C.: Carnegie Institution of Washington, Division of Historical Research.

Redfield, Robert, and Alfonso Villa Rojas

1934 *Chan Kom: A Maya Village.* Carnegie Institution of Washington Publication 448. Washington, D.C.: Carnegie Institution of Washington.

Riese, Berthold

1984 Hel Hieroglyphs. In *Phoneticism in Mayan Hieroglyphic Writing.* Edited by John S. Justeson and Lyle Campbell, pp. 263–286. Publication no. 9. Albany: Institute for Me-

soamerican Studies, State University of New York at Albany.

Ringle, William M.

1988 *Of Mice and Monkeys: The Value and Meaning of T1016, the God C Hieroglyph.* Research Reports on Ancient Maya Writing, no. 18. Washington, D.C.: Center for Maya Research.

Robicsek, Francis

1978 *The Smoking Gods: Tobacco in Maya Art, History, and Religion.* Norman: University of Oklahoma Press.

Rosny, León de

1856 *Collection d'anciennes peintures mexicaines.* Paris: Maisonneuve et Cie.

1860 *Les écritures figuratives et hiéroglyphiques des différents peuples anciens et modernes.* Paris: Maisonneuve et Cie.

1864 *Collection d'anciennes peintures mexicaines (hiéroglyphes mexicains), publié avec des notices descriptives.* Paris. [Glass (1957b:690) cites this as a possible second edition of Rosny 1856.]

1887 *Codex Peresianus. Manuscrit hiératique des anciens Indiens de l'Amérique Centrale conservé à la Bibliothèque Nacionale de Paris. Publié en coleurs avec une introduction. . . .* Paris: Bureau de la Société Américaine. [Lithographic edition with errors of omission caused by manipulation of the base photographs.]

1888 *Codex Peresianus. Manuscrit hiératique des anciens Indiens de l'Amérique Centrale conservé à la Bibliothèque Nacionale de Paris, avec une introduction . . . seconde édition imprimée en noir.* Paris: Bureau de la Société Américaine. [Unretouched images make this the most accurate of the early reproductions.]

Roys, Ralph L.

1933 *The Book of Chilam Balam of Chumayel.* Carnegie Institution of Washington Publication 436. Washington, D.C.: Carnegie Institution of Washington.

1949a *Guide to the Codex Pérez.* Contributions to American Anthropology and History, no. 49. Publication 585. Washington, D.C.: Carnegie Institution of Washington.

1949b *The Prophecies for the Maya Tuns or Years in the Books of Chilam Balam of Tizimin and Mani.* Contributions to American Anthropology and History, no. 51. Publication 585. Washington, D.C.: Carnegie Institution of Washington.

Schele, Linda

1974 Observations on the Cross Motif at Palenque. In *Primera Mesa Redonda de Palenque, Part 1*. Edited by Merle Greene Robertson, pp. 41–62. Pebble Beach, Calif.: Robert Louis Stevenson School, Pre-Columbian Art Research.

1976 Accession Iconography of Chan-Bahlum in the Group of the Cross at Palenque. In *The Art, Iconography, and Dynastic History of Palenque, Part III*. Edited by Merle Greene Robertson, pp. 9–34. Pebble Beach, Calif.: Robert Louis Stevenson School, Pre-Columbian Art Research.

Schellhas, Paul

1904 *Representations of Deities of the Maya Manuscripts*. Papers of the Peabody Museum of American Archaeology and Ethnology, Harvard University, vol. 4, no. 1. Cambridge: Peabody Museum.

Schultze Jena, Leonhard

1938 Bei den Azteken Mixteken und Tlapaneken der Sierra Madre del Sur. *Indiana*. Vol. 3. Jena: Verlag von Gustav Fischer.

Schwede, Rudolph

1912 *Uber das Papier der Maya-Codices u. einiger altmexikanischer Bilderhandschriften*. Dresden: Royal Saxonian Technical University of Dresden. [Pages 18–21 deal with the Paris Codex.]

Seler, Eduard

1902–1923 *Gesammelte Abhandlungen sur americanishen Sprach- und Altertumskunde*. 5 vols. Berlin: Verlag A. Ascher. Reprint. Graz, Austria: Akademische Druck- und Verlagsanstalt, 1960. [Selected works are translated into English in Bowditch 1939.]

1904 The Mexican Chronology with Special Reference to the Zapotec Calendar. *Bureau of American Ethnology Bulletin*, no. 28:11–55. [Also in Seler 1902–1923.]

Severin, Gregory M.

1981 *The Paris Codex: Decoding an Astronomical Ephemeris*. Transactions of the American Philosophical Society, vol. 71, pt. 5. Philadelphia: American Philosophical Society.

Shook, Edwin M.

1955 *Another Round Temple at Mayapan*. Department of Archaeology Current Reports, no. 27. Washington, D.C.: Carnegie Institution of Washington.

Sky Publishing Corporation

1980 *SC1 Constellation Chart, Equatorial Region—Epoch 1925*. Cambridge.

Smailus, Ortwin

1975 *El Maya-Chontal de Acalan: Análisis lingüístico de un documento de los años 1610–1612*. Centro de Estudios Mayas, no. 9. Mexico City: Universidad Autónoma de México.

Solís Alcalá, Ermilio

1949 *Códice Pérez. Traducción libre del Maya al Castellano*. Mérida: Ediciones de la Liga de Acción Social.

Sosa, John R.

1985 The Maya Sky, the Maya World: A Symbolic Analysis of Yucatec Maya Cosmology. Ph.D. diss., State University of New York at Albany.

Spinden, Herbert J.

1913 *A Study of Maya Art, Its Subject Matter and Historical Development*. Memoirs of the Peabody Museum of American Archaeology and Ethnology, Harvard University, vol. 6. Cambridge: Peabody Museum. [Reprint. New York: Dover, 1975.]

1916 The Question of the Zodiac in America. *American Anthropologist* 18:53–80.

1924 *The Reduction of Mayan Dates*. Papers of the Peabody Museum of American Archaeology and Ethnology, Harvard University, vol. 6, no. 4. Cambridge: Peabody Museum.

1957 *Maya Art and Civilization*. Indian Hills, Colo.: Falcon's Wing Press.

Stuart, David

1987 *Ten Phonetic Syllables*. Research Reports on Ancient Maya Writing, no. 14. Washington, D.C.: Center for Maya Research.

1989 The Maya Artist, An Epigraphic and Iconographic Study. Senior Thesis, Department of Art and Archaeology, Princeton University.

Stuart, George

1986 Los Códices Mayas. *Archaeoastronomy* 9 (1–4): 164–176.

Sullivan, Paul

1989 *Unfinished Conversations: Mayas and Foreigners Between Two Wars*. New York: Alfred A. Knopf.

Taube, Karl

1988a A Prehispanic Maya Katun Wheel. *Journal of Anthropological Research* 44 (2): 183–203.

1988b   The Ancient Yucatec New Year Festival: The Liminal Period in Maya Ritual and Cosmology. Ph.D. diss., Yale University.

1989a   *Itzam Cab Ain: Caimans, Cosmology, and Calendrics in Postclassic Yucatán.* Research Reports on Ancient Maya Writing, no. 26. Washington, D.C.: Center for Maya Research.

1989b   The Maize Tamale in Classic Maya Diet, Epigraphy, and Art. *American Antiquity* 54 (1): 31–51.

1992   *The Major Gods of Ancient Yucatan.* Studies in Pre-Columbian Art and Archaeology, no. 32. Washington, D.C.: Dumbarton Oaks.

Tedlock, Barbara

1982   *Time and the Highland Maya.* Albuquerque: University of New Mexico Press.

1992   *Time and the Highland Maya: Revised Edition.* Albuquerque: University of New Mexico Press.

Thomas, Cyrus

1882   *A Study of the Manuscript Troano.* U.S. Department of the Interior Contributions to North American Ethnology, vol. 5, no. 3. Washington, D.C.: Government Printing Office.

1897–1898   Numeral Systems of Mexico and Central America. In *Nineteenth Annual Report of the Bureau of American Ethnology,* part 2, pp. 853–955. Washington, D.C.: Government Printing Office.

Thompson, J. Eric S.

1927   *A Correlation of the Mayan and European Calendars.* Field Museum of Natural History Anthropological Series, vol. 17, no. 1. Publication 241. Chicago: Field Museum of Natural History.

1934   *Sky Bearers, Colors, and Directions in Maya and Mexican Religion.* Contributions to American Archaeology, no. 10. Publication 436. Washington, D.C.: Carnegie Institution of Washington.

1937   *A New Method of Deciphering Yucatecan Dates with Special Reference to Chichén Itzá.* Contributions to American Archaeology, no. 22. Publication 483. Washington, D.C.: Carnegie Institution of Washington.

1941   *Maya Arithmetic.* Contributions to American Anthropology and History, no. 36. Publication 528. Washington, D.C.: Carnegie Institution of Washington.

1950   *Maya Hieroglyphic Writing: An Introduction.* Carnegie Institution of Washington Publication 589. Washington, D.C.: Carnegie Institution of Washington. [2d and 3d editions, 1960 and 1971, Norman: University of Oklahoma Press.]

1957   *Deities Portrayed on Censers at Mayapan.* Carnegie Institution of Washington Current Reports, no. 40. Cambridge: Carnegie Institution of Washington.

1965   Archaeological Synthesis of the Southern Maya Lowlands. In *Handbook of Middle American Indians.* Vol. 2, pt. 1. Edited by Robert Wauchop (General Editor) and Gordon Willey (Volume Editor), pp. 331–359. Austin: University of Texas Press.

1972   *A Commentary on the Dresden Codex A Maya Hieroglyphic Book.* Memoirs, vol. 93. Philadelphia: American Philosophical Society.

Tizimin, Book of Chilam Balam of
   See Mayer 1980

Tozzer, Alfred M.

1921   *A Maya Grammar with Bibliography and Appraisement of the Works Noted.* Papers of the Peabody Museum of American Archaeology and Ethnology, Harvard University, vol. 9. Cambridge: Peabody Museum.

1941   *Landa's Relación de las Cosas de Yucatán.* Papers of the Peabody Museum of American Archaeology and Ethnology, Harvard University, vol. 18. Cambridge: Peabody Museum.

1957   *Chichén Itzá and Its Cenote of Sacrifice: A Comparative Study of Contemporaneous Maya and Toltec.* Memoirs of the Peabody Museum of Archaeology and Ethnology, Harvard University, vols. 11 and 12. Cambridge: Peabody Museum.

Treiber, Hannelore

1987   *Studien zur Katunserie der Pariser Mayahandschrift.* Acta Mesoamericana, band 2. Edited by Eike Hinz, Ulrich Köhler, Hanns J. Prem, and Berthold Riese. Berlin: Verlag von Flemming. [Excellent black and white photos of pages 2–12.]

Ursua y Arismendi, Martín de

1697   Letter from Martín de Ursua y Arismendi to Crown, 30 July, 1697. Mexico 895. Archivo General de Indias, Seville.

van der Loo, Peter L.

1987   *Códices costumbres continuidad: Un estudio de la religión Mesoamericana.* Indiaanse Studies 2. Leiden: Archeologisch Centrum Rijksuniversiteit te Leiden.

Vienna Dictionary
See Mengin 1972

Villa Rojas, Alfonso

1945   *The Maya of East Central Quintana Roo.* Carnegie Institution of Washington Publication 559. Washington, D.C.: Carnegie Institution of Washington.

1978   *Los elegidos de dios: Etnografía de los mayas de Quintana Roo.* Colección de Antropología Social, no. 56. Mexico City: Instituto Nacional Indigenista.

Villacorta C., J. Antonio, and Carlos A. Villacorta

1930   *Códices Mayas. Reproducidos y desarrollados por J. Antonio Villacorta C. y Carlos A. Villacorta.* Guatemala: Tipografía Nacional. [This work first appeared in sequential parts, each containing sixteen codex pages plus respective diagrams, in fourteen numbers of the *Anales de la Sociedad de Geografía e Historia,* published in Guatemala from March 1930 (vol. 6, no. 3) to June 1933 (vol. 9, no. 4). Although the title page of the whole work bears the title page date of 1930, it did not actually appear until late 1933, as indicated on the cover wrappers. Reprints of this edition appeared in 1976 and 1977.]

Willard, Theodore A.

1933   *The Codex Pérez: An Ancient Mayan Hieroglyphic Book.* Photographic facsimile. Glendale, Calif.: Arthur H. Clarke.

Zimmermann, Günter

1954   Notas para la historia de los manuscritos Mayas. *Yan* 3:62–64.

Index

INDEX